Teach Me to Pray
Andrew Murray

BOOKS BY ANDREW MURRAY

Abiding in Christ
The Believer's School of Prayer
The Blood of Christ
Divine Healing
Humility
Living a Prayerful Life
Mighty Is Your Hand (edited by David Hazard)
The Ministry of Intercessory Prayer
The Path to Holiness
Raising Your Child to Love God
The Spirit of Christ
Teach Me to Pray
Waiting on God

Teach Me to Pray
Andrew Murray

BETHANYHOUSE
Minneapolis, Minnesota

Published by Bethany House Publishers
A Ministry of Bethany Fellowship International
11400 Hampshire Avenue South
Bloomington, Minnesota 55438
www.bethanyhouse.com

Printed in the United States of America by
Bethany Press International, Bloomington, Minnesota 55438

Library of Congress Cataloging-in-Publication Data

Murray, Andrew, 1828-1917.
    Teach me to pray : classic devotions edited for today's reader / by
Andrew Murray. — Rev. and updated.
        p. cm.
Rev. ed. of: The believer's school of prayer. 1982.
    ISBN 0-7642-2596-0 (pbk.)
    1. Prayer—Christianity. I. Murray, Andrew, 1828-1917. Believer's
school of prayer. II. Title.
    BV210.3 .M875   2002
    248.3'2—dc21   2002002803

Preface

Of all the promises connected with the command "Abide in me," there is none higher and none that more quickly brings the confession "Not that I have already obtained all this, or have already been made perfect" (Philippians 3:12), than this: "If you remain in me . . . *ask whatever you wish, and it will be given you*" (John 15:7). Power with God is the highest attainment of the abiding life.

Of all the Christlike traits, none is greater and more glorious than conformity to Him in the work that engages Him without ceasing in the Father's presence: His all-prevailing intercession. The more we abide in Him and grow in His likeness, the more His priestly life will work in us, and the more our life will become what His is: one that intercedes for others.

"[You] have made us kings and priests to our God" (Revelation 5:10). From both the king and the priest flow power, influence, and blessing. In the king, power comes down; in the priest, power rises and prevails with God. In our blessed Priest-King, Jesus Christ, the kingly power is founded on the priestly "*He is able* to save completely . . . *because* he always lives to intercede for them" (Hebrews 7:25). In believers, His priests and kings, this is also true. Through intercession, the church finds and exercises its highest power. Also through intercession, each member of the church proves his descent from Israel, who as a prince had power with God and with people and prevailed.

Teach Me to Pray has been written because of a deep conviction that the place and power of prayer in the Christian life has not been fully understood. As long as we look at prayer chiefly as the means of maintaining our own Christian life, we cannot fully know what it is intended to be. But when we learn to regard it as the most important work entrusted to us and as the root and strength of all other work, then we understand that there is nothing we need more than to study and practice the art of praying in the correct manner.

In the progressive teaching of our Lord about prayer and the wonderful promises given on His last night on earth (John 14:16) concerning the works we are to do in His name and the fruit we are to bear, one thing is clear: Only when the church yields itself to this holy work of intercession can it expect the power of Christ to be manifested on its behalf. It is my prayer that God will use this book to show His children the wonderful place of power and influence He longs and waits for us to occupy and for which a weary world also waits.

The Father longs to hear the prayer of faith, to give us whatever we ask for in Jesus' name. We tend to limit the great love and promises of our God. It seems we cannot read the simplest and clearest statements of our Lord without adding qualifying clauses. The church needs to learn that God intends that prayer have an answer! We have not yet fully conceived what God will do for the one who truly believes his prayer is heard. The truth that *God hears prayer* is universally admitted, but very few understand its full meaning or experience its full power. If anyone is motivated enough to take the Master's promises simply and literally as they stand, my object in writing this book will have been attained.

Multitudes have found unspeakable blessing in learning how completely Christ is our very life and how He undertakes to be and to do everything in us that we need Him to be and to do. The question remains as to whether we have learned to apply this truth to our prayer life. Many complain that they lack power to pray in faith, to pray the effective prayer that accomplishes something. But Jesus is waiting, longing, to teach us this. In heaven He ever lives to pray for us. His life in us is an always-praying life, if we only trust Him for it. Christ teaches us to pray not only by example, instruction, command, and promises but also by showing us that *He is our ever-living intercessor.* When we believe this and abide in Him for our prayer life too, our fears of not being able to pray correctly will vanish. We will joyfully and triumphantly trust our Lord to teach us to pray and to be the life and power of our prayers.

May God open our eyes to see what the glorious ministry of intercession is to which we as His royal priesthood have been set apart. May He help us to believe what mighty influence our prayers can have, and may all fear of being unable to fulfill our calling vanish as we grasp the truth that Jesus is living in us and interceding for us.

—Andrew Murray

Contents

Chapter 1

The Only Teacher

*One day Jesus was praying in a certain place. When he
finished, one of his disciples said to him,
"Lord, teach us to pray."*

Luke 11:1

The disciples had been with Christ and had seen Him pray.
They had learned to understand something of the connection between His public life and His private life of prayer.
They had learned to believe in Him as a Master in the art of
prayer—none could pray like Him. So they came to Him
with the request "Lord, teach us to pray." In hindsight they
surely would have told us that few things surpassed what He
taught them about prayer.

On this day in Luke's account, the disciples felt the need
to repeat their common request: "Lord, teach us to pray." As
we grow in the Christian life, the concept of Christ's never-
failing intercession becomes increasingly wonderful. It stirs
in us a desire to be *like Christ* in His intercession.

As we see Him pray, and we remember that no one can
pray or teach like Him, we agree with the disciples and say,
"Lord, teach *us* to pray." As we think about the fact that He

is our very life, we feel assured that we have but to ask and He will be delighted to take us into closer fellowship with himself and to teach us to pray as He prays.

Let us say today as they did of old, "Lord, teach us to pray." As we meditate we will find each word of our petition full of meaning.

Prayer is what we need to be taught. Though in its beginnings prayer is so simple that even a small child can pray, it is at the same time the highest and holiest work to which anyone can rise. It is fellowship with the unseen and most holy One. The powers of the eternal world have been placed at its disposal. It is the very essence of true religion. It is the channel of all blessings and the secret of power and life. Through prayer, God has given to everyone the right to take hold of Him and His strength. It is on prayer that promises wait for their fulfillment, the kingdom for its coming, and the glory of God for its full revelation.

We know, however, that we are weak and unfit for this holy task. Only the Spirit of God can enable us to do it as it should be done. How quickly we are deceived into resting in the *form* of prayer, while the power is missing! Our early training, the teaching of the church, the influence of habit, the stirring of the emotions—any of these can lead to prayer that has virtually no spiritual power. To be taught true prayer—that which takes hold of God's strength and to which the gates of heaven are opened wide—who would not cry, "O for someone to teach me how to truly pray!"

Jesus has actually opened a school for training His redeemed who seek to have power in prayer. Let us enter it with the petition "Lord, this is what we need to be taught! Please teach us to pray like this!"

We read in your Word about the power your believing

people of old had in prayer and the mighty wonders that were done in answer to them. If this took place under the old covenant, in the time of preparation, how much more should it take place in these days of fulfillment as a sure sign of your presence in their midst. We have heard the promises given to your apostles about the power of prayer in your name. And we have seen how gloriously they experienced the truth of those promises. We also know that the same promises can become true for us. Even today we consistently hear about what glorious tokens of your power you give to those who trust you completely. We know that all those who pray and receive have the same desires we have. Teach *us* to pray as they do. We know the promises are as much for us as for them. Teach *us* to pray so that we may receive answers to our prayers. You have entrusted your work to us as well. On our prayers the coming of your kingdom also depends. In our prayer too you can glorify your name. Yes, Lord, we offer ourselves as learners. We would be taught of you.

At first there is no work that appears so simple as prayer. But now we feel the need of being *taught* to pray. Later we may see that there is no task that is more difficult. The confession is forced from our lips that we do not know how to pray as we ought. It is true we have God's Word with its clear and sure promises, but sin has darkened our minds so that we do not always know how to apply the Word. In spiritual things we do not always seek the most important things, or we fail in praying according to the law of the sanctuary. In temporal things we are still less able to avail ourselves of the wonderful liberty our Father has given us to ask for what we need. Even when we know what to ask, how much is still needed to make our prayer acceptable? It must be to the glory of God, in full surrender to His will, in full assurance of faith, in the name of Jesus, and with a perseverance that refuses to be denied. All this must be learned. And it can only be learned in the school of much prayer, for it is practice that makes perfect. Amid the painful consciousness of ignorance and unworthiness, and in the struggle between believing and doubting, the heavenly art of effective prayer is learned. Because even when we do not remember it, there is One—the beginner and finisher of our faith and prayer— who watches over our praying and sees to it that *all who trust Him for it* shall be carried through to perfection in this school. Let the deep undertone of all our prayer be the teachableness that comes from our own sense of ignorance and faith in Him as a perfect teacher. Then we shall be taught. We will learn to pray in power. We may depend upon it; He *teaches* us to pray.

A pupil needs a teacher who knows his work and has the gift of teaching, who in patience and love will condescend to the pupil's level. Jesus is all this and much more. No one can teach like Jesus. It is Jesus, praying himself, who teaches us to pray. He knows what prayer is. He learned it in the trials and tears of His earthly life. In heaven it is still His beloved work; His life there is intercession. Nothing delights Him more than to find those whom He can take with Him into the Father's presence. He can clothe them with power to pray down God's blessing on those around them. He can train them to be His fellow workers in the intercession by which the kingdom is to be revealed on earth. He knows how to teach through the urgency of felt need and by the confidence joy inspires. He teaches by His Word and by the testimony of other believers who know what it is to have their prayer heard. By His Holy Spirit He has access to our heart, and either shows us the sin that hinders our prayer or the assurance that we are pleasing to God. He teaches not only by thoughts of what to ask or how to ask but also by breathing within us the very spirit of prayer, by living within us as the Great Intercessor. In awe and joy we ask, "Who teaches like Him?"

Jesus did not teach His disciples how to preach but how to pray. To know how to speak to God is more vital than knowing how to speak to men. It is power with God not man that is of supreme importance.

As we meditate on the words He spoke while on earth, let us give ourselves especially to His teaching on the art of prayer. We can have the fullest confidence that with such a teacher we will make good progress. Let us not only meditate but also pray and wait at the foot of the throne to be trained for the work of intercession—in the assurance that even with our stammering He is beautifully carrying on His work. He will breathe into us His own life, which is prayer itself. As He makes us partakers of His righteousness and of His life, He will make us partakers of His intercession. As the members of His body, as a holy priesthood, we shall take part in His priestly work of pleading and prevailing with God for men. Ignorant and feeble as we are, Lord, teach us to pray.

Blessed Lord, you ever live to pray, and you can teach me to live to pray. You make me share your glory in heaven through my praying without ceasing and by my standing as a priest in the presence of my God.

Lord Jesus, I confess I do not know how to pray as I ought. Teach me to wait on you and in so doing give you time to train me to pray. May a deep sense of my ignorance, of the wonderful privilege and power of prayer, and of the need of the Holy Spirit as the Spirit of prayer, lead me to surrender my thoughts of what I think I know. Draw me to kneel before you in true teachableness and poverty of spirit.

Fill me, Lord, with confidence that with you as my teacher, I will learn to pray. With Jesus as my teacher—He who ever prays to the Father and by His prayer rules the destinies of His church and the world—I need not be afraid. As much as I need to know of the mysteries of the prayer world, you will unfold for me. And when it is not for me to know, you will teach me to be strong in faith, giving glory to God.

Blessed Lord, you will not put to shame your scholar who trusts you, nor will I by your grace put you to shame. Amen.

Chapter 2

The True Worshipers

Yet a time is coming and has now come when the true worshipers will worship the Father in spirit and truth, for they are the kind of worshipers the Father seeks. God is spirit, and his worshipers must worship in spirit and in truth.

John 4:23–24

Jesus' words to the woman of Samaria are His first recorded teaching on prayer. They give us some wonderful first glimpses into the world of prayer. The Father *seeks* worshipers. Our worship satisfies His loving heart and is a joy to Him. He seeks *true worshipers* but does not find many. True worship is that which is *in spirit and truth*. The Son has come to open the way for this worship and to teach it to us. One of our first lessons in the school of prayer must be to understand what it means to pray in the spirit and in truth and to know *how* we can do it.

To the woman of Samaria our Lord spoke of a threefold worship. There is, first, the unlearned worship of the Samaritans: "You Samaritans worship what you do not know" (John 4:22). The second, the intelligent worship of the Jew, having the true knowledge of God: "We worship what we do know, for salvation is from the Jews" (John 4:22). And then the new spiritual worship that He himself has come to introduce: "Yet a time is coming and has now come when the true worshipers will worship the Father in spirit and truth" (John 4:23). From the connection, it is evident that the words "in spirit and truth" do not mean, as is often thought, "earnestly, from the heart, in sincerity." The Samaritans had the five books of Moses and some knowledge of God; there was doubtless more than one among them who honestly and earnestly sought God in prayer. The Jews had the full revelation of God in His Word as had until then been given; there were among them godly men who called upon God with their whole hearts. But worshiping "in spirit and truth" was not yet fully realized. Jesus says, "Yet a time is coming and has now come" (John 4:23); it is only in and through Him that the worship of God will be in spirit and truth.

Among Christians we can still find the three classes of worshipers: some, in their ignorance, hardly know what they are asking. They pray earnestly but receive little. Others, with more knowledge, try to pray with all their mind and heart—often most earnestly, but do not attain the full blessing of worship in spirit and truth. We must ask our Lord Jesus to take us into this third class; we must be taught of Him how to worship in spirit and truth. This alone is spiritual worship. This makes us the kind of worshipers the Father seeks. In prayer, everything depends on our understanding and practicing worship in spirit and truth.

"God is *spirit*, and his worshipers must worship *in spirit* and in truth" (John 4:24). The first thought suggested here by the Master is that there must be harmony between God and His worshipers; as God is, so must His worship be. This obeys a principle that prevails throughout the universe: we look for correspondence between an object and the organ or body to which it reveals or yields itself. The eye has an inner fitness for the light, the ear for sound. The man who would truly worship God, who would find, know, possess, and enjoy God must be in harmony with Him and have the capacity for receiving Him. Because God *is spirit*, we must worship Him *in spirit*. As God is, so His worshiper must be.

What does this mean? The woman asked our Lord whether Samaria or Jerusalem was the true place of worship. He answers that from this time on worship is no longer to be limited to a certain place: "Believe me, woman, *a time is coming* when you will worship the Father neither on this mountain nor in Jerusalem" (John 4:21). As God is spirit—not bound by space or time but in His infinite perfection always and everywhere the same—so His worship must no longer be confined by place or form, but be spiritual as God himself is spiritual. This is a lesson of deep importance. How much our Christianity suffers because it is confined to certain times and places! A man who seeks to pray earnestly in the church or in his prayer corner spends the greater part of the week or the day in a spirit entirely at variance with the spirit in which he prayed. His worship was the work of a fixed place or hour and not of his whole being. *God is spirit.* He is the everlasting and unchangeable one. What He is, He is always and everywhere. Our worship must also be in spirit and in truth. His worship must be the spirit of our life. Our life must be worship in spirit as God is spirit.

The second thought is that this worship in the spirit must come from God himself. God is spirit; He alone has spirit to give. It was for this He sent His Son to fit us for such spiritual worship by giving us the Holy Spirit. It is of His own work that Jesus speaks when He says twice, "A time is coming," and then He adds, "and has now come" (John 4:21, 23). He came to baptize with the Holy Spirit; the Spirit could not be poured forth until He was glorified (John 1:33; 7:37–38; 16:7). It was when He had made an end of sin and entered into the Holiest of all with His blood, that He there on our behalf *received* the Holy Spirit (Acts 2:33) and could send Him down to us. It was when Christ had redeemed us, and we in Him had received the position of children, that the Father sent forth the Spirit of His Son into our hearts to cry, "Abba, Father." The worship in spirit means the worship of the Father in the Spirit of Christ, the Spirit of sonship.

This is the reason Jesus here uses the name *Father* (John 4:21, 23). We never find one of the Old Testament saints who personally appropriates the name of child or calls God his Father. The worship *of the Father* is only possible to those to whom the Spirit of the Son has been given. The worship *in spirit* is only possible to those to whom the Son has revealed the Father, and who have received the spirit of sonship. It is only Christ who opens the way and teaches worship in the Spirit.

In truth does not only mean *in sincerity.* Nor does it only signify in accordance with the truth of God's Word. The expression is one of deep and divine meaning. Jesus is "the only-begotten of the Father, *full* of grace and *truth*" (John 1:14 NKJV). "For the law was given through Moses; grace and *truth came* through Jesus Christ" (John 1:17). Jesus says, "*I am . . . the truth* and the life" (John 14:6). In the Old Testament all was shadow and promise. Jesus brought and gives the reality, *the substance*, of things hoped for. In Him the blessings and powers of eternal life are our actual possession and experience. Jesus is full of grace and truth. The Holy Spirit is the spirit of truth. Through Him the grace that is in

Jesus is ours in deed and truth, a positive communication out of the divine life. So worship in spirit is worship *in truth*, actual living fellowship with God, with a real correspondence and harmony between the Father, who is a spirit, and the child praying in the Spirit.

The woman of Samaria could not immediately understand what Jesus said to her. Pentecost was needed to reveal its full meaning. We are hardly prepared at our entrance into the school of prayer to grasp such teaching. We will understand it better later on. Let us take the lesson as He gives it. We are carnal and cannot give God the worship He seeks. But Jesus came to give us the Spirit. He has given Him to us. Let the disposition in which we set ourselves to pray be as Christ's words have taught us. Let there be the deep confession of our inability to give God the worship that is pleasing to Him, the childlike teachableness that waits on Him for instruction, and the simple faith that yields itself to the breath of the Spirit. Above all, let us hold on to the blessed truth that the knowledge of the fatherhood of God, the revelation of His infinite fatherliness in our hearts, the faith in the infinite love that gives us His Son and His Spirit to make us children, is indeed the secret of prayer in the spirit and in truth. This is the new and living way Christ has opened up for us. To have Christ the Son and *the Spirit of the Son* dwelling within us and revealing the Father makes us true spiritual worshipers.

Blessed Lord, I adore the love with which you taught a woman who had refused you a cup of water what the worship of God must be. I rejoice in the assurance that you will no less instruct your disciple who comes to you with a heart that longs to pray in the spirit and in truth. O Holy Master, teach me this blessed secret.

Teach me that spiritual worship is not of man, but comes from you; that it is not something of times and seasons but rather the outflowing of a life in you. Teach me to draw near to you in prayer with a deep awareness of my ignorance and of my having nothing in myself to offer, and at the same time of the provision that you, my Savior, make for the Spirit's breathing into my childlike stammering. I bless you that in you I am a child and have a child's liberty of access, that in you I have the spirit of sonship and of worship in truth. Teach me, above all, blessed Son of the Father, how it is the revelation of the Father that gives us confidence in prayer. Let the infinite fatherliness of God's heart be my joy and strength for a life of prayer and of worship. Amen.

Chapter 3

Alone With God

But when you pray, go into your room, close the door and pray to your Father, who is unseen. Then your Father, who sees what is done in secret, will reward you.

Matthew 6:6

Jesus gave His first disciples their first public teaching in the Sermon on the Mount. He expounded to them the kingdom of God, its laws and its life. In that kingdom God is not only King but also Father. He not only gives all but is all. The knowledge and fellowship of Him alone is its own reward. So the revelation of prayer and the prayer life was a part of His teaching concerning the new kingdom He came to set up. Moses gave neither command nor regulation with regard to prayer. Even the prophets say very little in direct reference to the practice of prayer. *It is Christ who teaches us to pray.*

The first thing the Lord teaches His disciples is that they must have a secret place for prayer. Everyone must have some solitary spot where he can be alone with God. Every teacher must have a schoolroom. Jesus is our teacher in the school of prayer. He has already taught us at Samaria that worship is no longer confined to times and places, but that true spiritual worship is something of the spirit and of the life. The whole man must in his whole life worship in spirit and truth. But He still sees it as important that each one choose a location where he can daily meet with Him. That inner room, that solitary place, is Jesus' schoolroom. That spot could be anywhere. It may even change from day to day if we have to move for the sake of family or schedules, but there must be a secret place and a quiet time in which the student places himself in the Master's presence to be prepared by Him to worship the Father. Jesus comes to us in that place and teaches us to pray.

A teacher wants his schoolroom to be bright and attractive, light and airy, a place where pupils want to come and love to stay. In the Sermon on the Mount, Jesus seeks to set the place of prayer before us in its most attractive light. We soon notice the most important thing He has to tell us about our waiting there. Three times He uses the name *Father*: "Pray to *your Father* ... *your Father* ... will reward you" (Matthew 6:6); "*Your Father* knows what you need before you ask him" (Matthew 6:8). The first need in private prayer is that we must meet our Father. The light that shines in the prayer closet must be the light of the Father's countenance. The fresh air from heaven with which Jesus would have it filled—the atmosphere in which we are to breathe and pray—is God's Father-love, God's infinite fatherliness. Thus each thought or petition we breathe will be simple, hearty, childlike trust in the Father. This is how the Master teaches us to pray. He brings us into the Father's living presence. In this atmosphere our prayers will accomplish much.

"Pray to your Father, who is unseen" (Matthew 6:6). God hides himself from the carnal eye. If in worship we are primarily occupied with our own thoughts and exercises, we will not meet Him who is spirit. But to the one who withdraws himself from all that is of the world and the flesh and prepares to wait upon God alone, the Father will reveal himself. As we forsake and shut out the life of the world and surrender ourselves to be led of Christ into the secret of God's presence, the light of the Father's love will rise upon us. The privacy of the inner room and the closed door, the entire separation from all around us, is an image of that inner spiritual sanctuary, the secret of God's tabernacle within the veil, where our spirit truly comes into contact with the invisible One. So at the very outset of our search after the secret of effective prayer, we are taught that it is in the private room alone with the Father that we will learn to pray correctly. In the words "The Father who is unseen," Jesus teaches us where He is waiting for us, where He is always to be found.

Christians often complain that private prayer is not what it should be. They feel weak and full of sin. Their hearts seem cold and dark. It is as if they have little to pray about, and not much faith or joy. They are discouraged and kept from prayer by the thought that they cannot come to the Father as they ought to or as they wish to. But precisely when your heart is cold and prayerless, is when you should go to the loving Father. As a father pities his children, so the Lord pities you. Do not think how little you have to bring God but how much He wants to give to you. Look into His face. Think of His tender, compassionate love. Tell Him how sinful and cold and dark you feel. The Father's loving heart will give you light and warmth. Do what Jesus says. Shut the door and pray to your Father who is unseen.

"Then your Father, who sees what is done in secret, will reward you" (Matthew 6:6). Jesus assures us that secret prayer will not be fruitless. Its blessing will be seen in our life. In secret, alone with God, if we entrust our life before men to Him, He will reward us openly. He will see to it that the answer to our prayer is manifested in His blessing upon us. Our Lord would teach us that just as God meets us in secret with infinite fatherliness and faithfulness, so we should have the childlike simplicity of faith and confidence that our prayer will be heard.

"Anyone who comes to [God] must believe that he . . . rewards those who earnestly seek him" (Hebrews 11:6). The blessing of the private place does not depend on the strong or fervent feeling with which I pray but upon the love and the power of the Father to whom I entrust my needs. Remember, your Father sees and hears in secret. Go there and remain; come out with confidence that He will reward you. Trust Him for it. Depend upon Him. Prayer to the Father is not in vain. He *will* reward you openly.

To confirm this faith in the Father-love of God, Christ speaks a third word: "Your Father knows what you need before you ask him" (Matthew 6:8). At first sight it might appear as if this thought makes prayer unnecessary. God knows far better than we do what we need. But as we get a deeper insight into what prayer really is, this truth will help to strengthen our faith. It will teach us that we do not need, as the heathen do, to use many words and urgent pleas to compel an unwilling God to listen to us. It will lead to a holy thoughtfulness and silence in prayer as we ask, "Does my Father really know that I need this?" When once the Spirit gives certainty that our request, according to the Word, is needed for God's glory, we can say with confidence, "My Father knows I need what I ask." If there is any delay in the answer, it will teach us to hold on in quiet perseverance.

Father! You *know* I need it. Christ, our teacher, wants to cultivate the blessed liberty and simplicity of a child in us as we draw near to God. Let us look up to the Father until His Spirit works it in us. When we are sometimes in danger of being so occupied with fervent, urgent petitions as to forget that the Father knows and hears, let us remain still and quietly say, "My Father sees, He hears, He knows." It will help our faith to claim the answer and to say, "We know that we have what we asked of him" (1 John 5:15).

Now take these lessons, practice them, and trust Him to perfect them in you. Dwell often in the private place, with the door shut against the world, your work, your responsibilities. There the Father waits for you. There Jesus will teach you to pray. To be alone in secret with the Father: may this be your highest joy. To be assured that the Father will openly reward the secret prayer so that it cannot remain unblessed—may this be your strength day by day. To know that the Father knows that you need what you ask will give you liberty to bring every need, in the assurance that your God will supply it according to His riches in glory in Christ Jesus.

Blessed Savior, with my whole heart I bless you for the appointment of the quiet place as the school where you meet each of your pupils alone and reveal the Father. My Lord, strengthen my faith in the Father's tender love and kindness so that my first instinctive thought, when sinful or troubled, may be to go where I know the Father waits for me and where prayer never goes unheard. Let the thought that He knows my need before I ask give me great restfulness of faith to trust that He will give what His child requires. Let the place of secret prayer become to me the most beloved place on earth.

Lord, hear me as I pray that you would everywhere bless the secret places of your believing people. Let your revelation of a Father's tenderness free young Christians from every thought that secret prayer is a duty or a burden and lead them to regard it as the highest privilege of their life, a joy and a blessing. Bring back all who are discouraged because they cannot find anything to bring to you in prayer. May they see that they only need to come with their emptiness to Him who has all to give—and delights to give. Let their one thought be not what they have to bring the Father but what the Father waits to give them.

Bless the inner room of all your servants as the place where God's truth and grace are revealed to them, where they are daily anointed with fresh oil, where their strength is renewed, and the blessings with which they are to bless their fellowmen are received in faith. Lord, draw us all to that place nearer to yourself and to the Father. Amen.

Chapter 4

The Model Prayer

*In this manner, therefore, pray: Our Father in heaven,
hallowed be Your name. Your kingdom come. Your will be
done on earth as it is in heaven. Give us
this day our daily bread.*

*And forgive us our debts, as we forgive our debtors. And do not
lead us into temptation, but deliver us from the evil one. For
Yours is the kingdom and the power
and the glory forever. Amen.*

Matthew 6:9–13 NKJV

Every teacher knows the power of example. He not only tells
the child what to do and how to do it but also shows him
that it really can be done. In condescension to our weakness,
our heavenly teacher has given us the very words to use as
we draw near to our Father. We have in them a form of
prayer in which there breathes the freshness and fullness of
eternal life: so simple that a child can lisp it, so divinely rich
that it takes in all that God can give. It is a form of prayer
that becomes the model and inspiration for all other prayer
and yet always draws us back to itself as the deepest utterance
of our souls before our God: *"Our Father in heaven . . ."* To

fully appreciate this word of adoration, remember that none of the saints in Scripture ever ventured to address God as their Father. The invocation places us at once in the center of the wonderful revelation that the Son came to make His Father our Father. It encompasses the mystery of redemption: Christ delivering us from the curse that we might become the children of God; the mystery of regeneration: the Spirit giving us new life by new birth; and the mystery of faith: even before their redemption is accomplished or understood, the word is given to the disciples in order to prepare them for the blessed experience yet to come.

The words are the key to the whole prayer; in fact, to all prayer. It takes time to study them. It will take eternity to fully understand them. The knowledge of God's Father-love is the first and simplest—but also the last and highest—lesson in the school of prayer. It is in personal relationship to the living God and conscious fellowship with Him that prayer begins. It is in the knowledge of God's fatherliness revealed by the Holy Spirit that the power of prayer will take root and grow. In the infinite tenderness and pity and patience of the infinite Father, in His loving readiness to hear and to help, the life of prayer has its joy. Let us take time for the Spirit to make these words spirit and truth to us, filling our heart and our life: "Our Father in heaven . . ." Here we are indeed within the veil, in the secret place of power where prayer always prevails.

"*Hallowed be Your name.*" While we ordinarily first bring our own needs to God in prayer, and then think of what belongs to God and His interests, the Master reverses the order. First, *Your* name, *Your* kingdom, *Your* will; then, give *us*, forgive *us*, lead *us*, and deliver *us*. The lesson is more important than we think. In true worship the Father must be first, must be all. The sooner I learn to forget myself in the desire that He might be glorified, the richer will be the blessing prayer will bring to me. No one ever loses by what he sacrifices for the Father.

There are two types of prayer: personal and intercessory. The latter ordinarily occupies the lesser part of our time and energy. But Christ has opened the school of prayer especially to train intercessors for the great work of bringing down, by their faith and prayer, the blessings of His work and love upon the world around them. Unless this is our aim, there can be no deep growth in prayer. A little child may ask of her father only what she needs for herself, although she soon learns to ask, "Give some for my sister too." But the grownup son who only lives for the father's interest and to care for his father's business, asks for bigger things and gets all that he asks. Jesus wants to train us in the blessed life of consecration and service in which our interests are all subordinate to the name, the kingdom, and the will of the Father. So let each act of adoration to "Our Father" be followed in the same breath by "*Your* name, *Your* kingdom, *Your* will."

"*Hallowed be Your name.*" What name? The name *Father*. The word *holy* is the central word of the Old Testament, the name *Father* of the New. All the holiness and glory of God are now to be revealed in this name of love. But how is the name to be hallowed? By God. "*I will show the holiness* of my great name . . . the name you have profaned*" (Ezekiel 36:23). Our prayer must be that in all and everywhere God himself would reveal the holiness and divine power, the hidden glory of the name *Father*. The Spirit of the Father is the *Holy Spirit*. Only when we yield ourselves to be led by Him, will His name be *hallowed* in our prayers and in our lives.

"*Your kingdom come.*" The Father is a king and has a

kingdom. The son and heir of a king has no higher ambition than the glory of his father's kingdom. In time of war or danger this becomes his passion. He can think of nothing else. The children of the Father are here in the enemy's territory, where the kingdom—which is in heaven—is not yet fully manifested. When they learn to hallow the Father-name, what is more natural than that they should long and cry with deep enthusiasm, "Your kingdom come"? The coming of the kingdom is the one great event on which the revelation of the Father's glory, the blessedness of His children, and the salvation of the world depends. The coming of the kingdom waits on our prayers. Shall we not join in the deep, longing cry of the redeemed: "Your kingdom come"?

"Your will be done on earth as it is in heaven." Too frequently this petition is applied only to *suffering* in connection with the will of God. In heaven God's will *is done*, and the Master teaches the child to ask that His will be done on earth as it is in heaven—in the spirit of adoring submission and ready obedience. Because the will of God is the glory of heaven, the doing of it is the blessedness of heaven. As His will is done, the kingdom of heaven enters the heart. Wherever faith has accepted the Father's love, obedience accepts the Father's will. Surrender to and prayer for a life of heaven-like obedience is the spirit of childlike prayer.

"Give us this day our daily bread." When the child has first yielded himself to the Father out of concern for His name, His kingdom, and His will, he has full liberty to ask for his daily bread. A master provides food for his servant, a general for his soldiers, a father for his child. Will not the Father in heaven provide for the child who has in prayer given himself up to His interests? In full confidence we may say, "Father, I live for your honor and your work. I know

you care for me." Consecration to God and His will gives wonderful liberty in prayer for temporal things, because the whole earthly life is given over to the Father's loving care.

"*And forgive us our debts, as we forgive our debtors.*" As bread is the first need of the body, so forgiveness is for the soul. The provision for the one is as sure as for the other. We are children, but we are also sinners. We owe our right of access to the Father's presence to the precious blood of Christ and the forgiveness it has won for us. Let us be careful that the prayer for forgiveness does not become a mere formality. *Only what is truly confessed is truly forgiven.* Let us in faith accept the forgiveness that is promised as a spiritual reality and an actual transaction between God and us. It is the entrance into all the privileges of His children. Such forgiveness as a living experience is impossible without a forgiving spirit toward others; because just as being *forgiven* expresses the heavenward relationship, so *forgiving* expresses the earthward relationship of God's child. When I pray, I must be able to say that I know of no one whom I do not sincerely love.

"*And do not lead us into temptation, but deliver us from the evil one.*" In these three petitions—our daily bread, the forgiveness of our sins, our being kept from all sin and the power of the Evil One—all our personal need is included. The prayer for bread and pardon must be accompanied by the total surrender to live in holy obedience to the Father's will and by believing prayer to be kept in everything from the power of the Evil One by the power of the indwelling Spirit.

Jesus wants us to pray this way to the Father in heaven. Let His name, His kingdom, His will have first place; then His providing, pardoning, and keeping love will be our portion. Let the Lord's Prayer guide you to the true child-life—the Father being all to and for the child. You will better understand how Father and child are one, and how the heart that begins its prayer with God's will and glory will have the power in faith to speak out its own requests too. Such prayer will be the fellowship and interchange of love, always bringing you back in trust and worship to Him who is not only the Beginning but the End. "For Yours is the kingdom and the power and the glory forever. Amen."

You who are the only-begotten Son, teach us to pray, "Our Father." Thank you, Lord, for these living blessed words that you have given to us. We thank you for the multitudes who in them have learned to know and worship the Father. Thank you for what they have been to us. Lord, it seems we need days and weeks in your school with each petition—so deep and full are they. But we look to you to lead us deeper into their meaning. Do it, we pray, for your name's sake.

Lord, you once said, "No one knows the Father except the Son and those to whom the Son chooses to reveal him" (Matthew 11:27). And again, "I have made you known to them, and will continue to make you known in order that the love you have for me may be in them and that I myself may be in them" (John 17:26). Lord Jesus, reveal the Father to us. Let His name, His infinite Father-love, the love with which He loved you, according to your prayer, be in us. Then shall we say truthfully, "Our Father!" Then we will obey your teaching, and the first spontaneous breathing of our heart will be, "Our Father, Your name, Your kingdom, Your will." Our needs and our sins and our temptations we will bring to Him in the confidence that the love of such a Father cares for all.

Blessed Lord, we are your students. We trust you. Teach us to pray. Amen.

Chapter 5

The Certainty of an Answer to Prayer

Ask and it will be given to you; seek and you will find; knock and the door will be opened to you. For everyone who asks receives; he who seeks finds; and to him who knocks, the door will be opened.

Matthew 7:7–8

When you ask, you do not receive, because you ask with wrong motives.

James 4:3

Our Lord returns to speak of prayer again in the Sermon on the Mount. The first time he told about the Father who is to be found in secret and rewards openly and gave us the pattern prayer (Matthew 6:5–15). Here He wants to teach us what all Scripture considers the most important thing in prayer: that it be heard and answered. He uses words that mean almost the same thing, and each time He repeats the promise distinctly: "It *will* be given to you; you *will* find; the door *will* be opened to you." Then he gives the law of the kingdom as the basis for such assurance: "For everyone who asks *receives*; he who seeks *finds*; and to him who knocks, the door *will be opened.*" In all this repetition, we can see that He wants to implant in our minds the truth that we may—and must—confidently expect an answer to our prayer. Next to the revelation of the Father's love, there is no more important lesson in the whole school of prayer than this: Everyone that asks receives.

A difference of meaning has been sought in the three words *ask, seek,* and *knock.* The first, ask, refers to the gifts we pray for. But I may ask for and receive a gift without the Giver. Seek is the word Scripture uses when speaking of looking for God himself. Christ assures me that I can find God. But it is not enough to find God in a time of need without also coming into an abiding fellowship with Him. Knock speaks of being admitted to dwell with Him and in Him. Asking and receiving the gift thus leads to seeking and finding the Giver. This again leads to the knocking and opening of the door to the Father's home and to His love. One thing is sure: the Lord wants us to believe with certainty that asking, seeking, and knocking will not be in vain. Receiving an answer, finding God, the opened heart and home of God, are the certain fruit of prayer.

It is significant that the Lord thought it necessary to repeat the truth in so many forms. It proves that He knows our hearts, how doubt and distrust toward God are natural to us, and how easily we are inclined to rest in prayer as a religious duty without expecting an answer. He knows too how, even when we believe that God hears our prayer, we still may feel believing prayer that claims God's promise to answer is something very spiritual, too high and difficult for the halfhearted disciple. So at the very outset of His instruction on prayer, He seeks to lodge this truth deep into their hearts: Prayer does accomplish much. Ask and you *will* receive; *everyone* that asks receives. This is the fixed eternal law of the kingdom. So if you ask and do not receive, it must be because there is something wrong or lacking in your prayer.

Persevere; let the Word and the Spirit teach you to pray in the right way and do not let go of the confidence He seeks to impart that everyone who asks receives an answer.

Christ has no greater stimulus to persevering prayer in His school than this. As a child has to prove a mathematical sum correct, so the proof that we have prayed correctly is *our answer*. If we have asked and not received, it is because we have not learned to pray in the right way. Let every learner in the school of Christ, therefore, believe the Master's promises to answer in all simplicity. He had good reasons for speaking so unconditionally. Let us beware of weakening the Word with our human wisdom. When He tells us heavenly things, let us believe Him. His Word will explain itself to him who believes it fully. If questions and difficulties arise, let us not seek to have them settled before we accept the Word. Rather let us entrust them all to Him. It is His work to solve them. Our work is to accept and hold fast His promise.

According to the Master's teaching, prayer has two sides: human and divine. The human side is the asking, the divine is the giving. Or to look at both from the human side, there is the asking and the receiving—the two halves that make up a whole. He tells us that we are not to rest without an answer, because it is the will of God—the rule in the Father's family—that every childlike believing petition is granted. If no answer comes, we are not to sit down in resignation and suppose that it is not God's will to give an answer. Something in the prayer must not be as God would have it: childlike and believing. We must seek for grace to pray in such a way that the answer comes. It is far easier for the flesh to submit without the answer than to yield itself to be searched and purified by the Spirit until it has learned to pray the prayer of faith.

One of the marks of the weakened state of the Christian life these days is that there are so many who rest content without specific answers to prayer. They pray daily, they ask many things, and trust that some of them will be heard, but know little of direct, definite answers to prayer as the rule of daily life. But this is what the Father wills. He seeks daily interaction with His children in listening to and granting their petitions. He wills that I should come to Him day by day with specific requests; He wills day-by-day to do for me what I ask. The saints of old learned to know God as the Living One by His answers to prayer and were stirred to praise and love (Psalms 34; 66; 19; 116:1). Our Teacher waits to imprint upon our minds that prayer and its answer—the child asking and the father giving—are inseparably linked.

Sometimes the answer is a refusal because the request is not according to God's Word, just as when Moses asked to enter Canaan. But there was an answer. God did not leave His servant in uncertainty as to His will. The gods of the heathen are dumb and cannot speak. Our Father lets His child know when He will not give him what he asks. Then the child can withdraw his petition, just as the Son did in Gethsemane. Both Moses the servant and Christ the Son knew that what they asked was not according to what the Lord had spoken; their prayers were humble supplications as to whether it was possible for the decision to be reversed. By His Word and Spirit, God will teach those who are teachable; give Him time and He will show them whether or not their request is according to His will. Let us withdraw the request if it is not according to God's mind. If it is, let us persevere until the answer comes. Prayer is appointed to us to obtain an answer. In prayer and its answer the interchange of love between the Father and His child takes place.

How deep the estrangement of our heart from God must be that we find it so difficult to grasp these promises. Although we may accept the words and believe their truth, the faith of the heart that fully trusts and rejoices in them comes slowly. Because our spiritual life is weak and our capacity for thinking God's thoughts frail, let us look to Jesus to teach us as only He can. If we take His words at face value and trust Him by His Spirit, He will make them life and power to us.

Let us decide to learn this lesson well and take these words as they were spoken. Do not let human reason weaken them. In due time Jesus will help us to understand them fully. Let us begin by believing them implicitly. Do not allow the experiences of your unbelief to be the measure of what your faith expects. In every situation let us hold to the joyful assurance that man's prayer on earth and God's answer from heaven are meant for each other. Trust Jesus to teach you to pray, so that the answer comes. He will do it if we believe His words: "Ask and it will be given to you."

Lord Jesus, teach me to understand and believe what you have promised. You know how my heart seeks to satisfy itself when no answer comes. Is my prayer in harmony with the Father's secret counsel? Is there something better you would give me? Is prayer as fellowship with you blessing enough without expecting an answer? But, Lord, I find in your teaching on prayer that you did not say these things; rather you said plainly that prayer may and must expect an answer. You have assured us that the child asks and the Father gives.

Lord, your words are faithful and true. If I do not receive, I must be praying with wrong motives. Perhaps I live too little in the Spirit, so that my prayer is too little of the Spirit, and the power for the prayer of faith is lacking.

Lord Jesus, teach me to pray in faith. Amen.

The Infinite Fatherliness
of God

*Which of you, if his son asks for bread, will give him a stone?
Or if he asks for a fish, will give him a snake? If you, then,
though you are evil, know how to give good gifts to your
children, how much more will your Father in heaven
give good gifts to those who ask him!*

Matthew 7:9–11

Our Lord confirms further what He said of the certainty of
an answer to prayer. To remove all doubt and show us on
what sure ground His promise rests, He appeals to a truth all
have seen and experienced here on earth. We are all children,
and know what we expected of our fathers. Any way we look
at it, it is a most natural thing for a father to hear his child.
And the Lord asks us to look up from our earthly parents—
of whom the best are but evil—and to calculate *how much
more* the heavenly Father will give good gifts to them that
ask Him. Jesus shows us that to the degree that God is
greater than sinful man, so should we base our assurance
that God will grant our childlike petitions. As God is to be

— 41 —

trusted more than man, *so much more certain* is it that our prayer will be heard of our Father in heaven.

This parable is simple and intelligible. Equally deep and spiritual is the teaching it contains. The Lord reminds us that the prayer of a child of God is influenced entirely by the relationship he has with his Parent. Prayer can exert that influence only when the child is living and walking in a loving relationship in the home and in the service of the Father. The power of the promise "Ask and it will be given to you" (Matthew 7:7) lies in that good relationship. Then the prayer of faith and its answer will be the natural result. Today the lesson is: Live as a child of God, and you may pray as a child with complete certainty of an answer.

What is the mark of a true child? The child who by choice forsakes his father's house and finds no pleasure in the presence and love of his father, but who still expects to ask and obtain what he wants, will surely be disappointed. On the contrary, he to whom the love and will of the father are the joy of his life will find that it is the father's joy to grant his requests. Scripture says, "Those who are *led* by the Spirit of God are sons of God" (Romans 8:14). The childlike privilege of asking for anything is inseparable from the childlike life under the leading of the Spirit. The one who yields himself to be led by the Spirit in his everyday life will be led by Him also in his prayers. He will find that father-like giving is the divine response to childlike living.

What is this childlike living on which childlike asking and believing are grounded? In the Sermon on the Mount our Lord teaches about the Father and His children. In it, the prayer-promises He gives are inseparably imbedded in the life precepts. They form one whole. He alone can count on the fulfillment of the promise who also accepts all that the Lord links with it.

In saying "Ask and it will be given to you" (Matthew 7:7), He implies: I give these promises to those whom I refer to in the Beatitudes (5:3–11). I have pictured their childlike poverty and purity and called them "sons of God" (5:9). I give them to children who "let [their] light shine before men, that they may . . . praise [their] Father in heaven" (5:16); to those who walk in love, "that [they] may be sons of [their] Father in heaven" (5:45), and who seek to be perfect "as [their] heavenly Father is perfect" (5:48); to those whose fasting and praying and almsgiving (6:1–18) is not done before men, but before "[their] Father, who sees what is done in secret" (6:6); who forgive as [their] Father forgives (6:14–15); who trust the heavenly Father for all earthly need, seeking first the kingdom of God and His righteousness (6:26–32); who not only say "Lord, Lord," but who do "the will of my Father who is in heaven" (7:21). Such are the children of the Father, and such is the life in the Father's love and service. To God's true children, answered prayers are certain and abundant.

This teaching may be discouraging to you. You may ask, Can we hope for answers to prayer if we must first be children like these passages describe? Yes, we can, if we remember the comforting comparison of father and child. A child is weak; children differ much in age and talents. But the Lord does not demand a perfect fulfillment of the law, only a childlike, wholehearted surrender to Him in obedience and truth. *Nothing more and nothing less.* The Father asks for the whole heart. And when He sees the child honestly, consistently seeking to live as a child, He will consider the prayer as the prayer of a child. If anyone studies the Sermon on the Mount and takes it at face value as his guide, he will find, in spite of weakness and failure, an ever-increasing liberty to claim fulfillment of the prayer-promises.

Jesus wants us to know the secret of effective prayer: a heart filled with the Father-love of God. It is not enough for us to know that God is our Father. He wants us to understand fully all that the name implies. Take the best earthly father you know. Think of the tenderness and love he gives to the request of his child and the joy with which he grants every reasonable desire. Then think in adoring worship of the infinite love and fatherliness of God, and consider with *how much more* tenderness and joy *He* sees us come and gives what we ask.

Is this beyond our understanding? Is it impossible for us to believe God's readiness to hear us? Then let the Holy Spirit shed abroad God's Father-love in our heart not only when we pray, but with a yielded heart and life that always dwells in that love. The child who only wants to know the love of his father when he asks for something will be disappointed. But the person who lets God be his Father always and in everything, who lives his whole life in the Father's presence and love, and who allows God in all the greatness of His compassion to be a Father to him, will experience in a glorious way that a life that trusts in God's infinite fatherliness and His continual answers to prayer are inseparable.

We begin to see why we know so little of daily answers to prayer and what the Lord's primary lesson is for us. It is rooted in the name *Father*. Instead of new and deeper insight into some of the mysteries of the prayer-world as we expected, Christ tells us that the highest lesson is to learn to say "Abba, Father!" (Romans 8:15) and "Our Father in heaven" (Matthew 6:9). The one who can address God with true sincerity and intimacy has the key to all prayer. Consider the compassion with which a father listens to his weak or sick child, the joy with which he hears his stammering child, the gentle patience with which he bears with a thoughtless child, and you will see as in a mirror the heart of your Father. The Word says, "*How much more* will your Father in heaven give good gifts to those who ask him!" (Matthew 7:11).

———————

The following excerpt is adapted from *Thoughts on Holiness* by Mark Guy Pearse (no publication data available).

"Our Father in heaven . . ." We generally speak it only as the utterance of a reverential homage. We think of it as an image borrowed from our earthly life, and only in some faint and shallow meaning to be used of God. We are afraid to take God as our own tender and companionable Father. We think of Him as our schoolmaster, or even further off than that, and knowing less about us—a superintendent, who knows nothing of us except through our lessons. His eyes are not on the scholar but on the book, and all must meet the standard equally.

But open the ears of your heart, timid child of God; let the words sink down into the innermost depths of your soul. Here is the starting point of holiness, in the love and patience and compassion of our heavenly Father. We are not to learn to be holy like a hard lesson at school, that we may make God think well of us; we are to learn it at home with the Father who longs to help us. God loves you not because you are clever, not because you are good, but because He is *your Father*. The cross of Christ does not make God love us; the cross is the outcome and measure of His love for us. He loves all His children—the clumsiest, the dullest, the poorest, even the outcast of society. His love lies at the back of every-thing, and we must rest upon that as the solid foundation of our Christian life, not growing up *into* that, but growing up *out of it.* We must begin there or our beginning will come to nothing. Seek to grasp this truth. We must go beyond our-selves to find any hope.

We need to comprehend the tenderness and helpfulness that lie in these words, and to rest upon them: "Our Father in heaven . . ." Speak them over to yourself until something of the wonderful truth is felt. It means that you are bound to God by the closest and gentlest relationship, that you have a right to His love and His power and His blessing—to His answers to your prayers. O the boldness with which we can draw near to Him! O the great things we have a right to ask of Him! He is our *Father.* It means that all His infinite love and patience and wisdom cover us and enfold us. In this relationship lies not only the possibility of holiness but infi-nitely more.

Here we are to begin, in the patient love of our Father. He knows each of us in all our peculiarities, in all our weak-nesses and difficulties. A master judges by the result, but our Father judges by the effort. Failure does not always mean fault or blame. He knows the cost of your efforts, and weighs them where others only measure. His love allows for the poor beginnings of the little ones, clumsy and unmeaning as they may be to others. All this and infinitely more lies in this blessed relationship with your Father. Do not fear to take it all as your own.

Blessed Lord, we know so little of the love of the Father. Although this is one of the first, simplest, and most glorious lessons in your school, you know that it is one of the hardest for us to learn. Teach us so to live with the Father that His love will be nearer, clearer, and dearer to us than the love of any earthly father. And let the assurance of His hearing our prayer be that much greater than the confidence we have in an earthly parent. Lord, show us that only our unchildlike distance from the Father hinders the answer to our prayer, and lead us on to the true life of God's children.

Let every prayer be breathed in the faith that as the heavens are higher than the earth, so God's Father-love and His readiness to give us what we ask surpass all we can think or conceive. Amen.

Chapter 7

The All-Comprehensive Gift

If you then, though you are evil, know how to give good gifts
to your children, how much more will your Father
in heaven give the Holy Spirit to those who ask him!

Luke 11:13

In the Sermon on the Mount, the Lord uttered His wonderful "how much more?" (Matthew 7:9–11). Here in Luke, where He repeats the question, there is a difference. Instead of speaking of giving *good gifts*, He says, "How much more will your Father in heaven give *the Holy Spirit*." He thus teaches us that the best of these gifts is the Holy Spirit, that in this gift all others are comprised. The Holy Spirit is the first of the Father's gifts and the one He delights most to bestow. The Holy Spirit is therefore the gift we ought to seek first.

We can easily understand the unspeakable worth of this gift. Jesus spoke of the Spirit as "the gift my Father promised" (Acts 1:4)—the one promise in which God's fatherhood is revealed. The best gift a good and wise father can bestow on a child is his own spirit. To reproduce in his child his own disposition and character is the great objective of a father in education. If the child is to know and understand his father and enter into all his plans for him, if he is to have his highest joy in the father and the father in him, the child must be of one mind and spirit with his father. So it is impossible to conceive of God bestowing any higher gift on His child than His own Spirit. God is what He is through His Spirit. The Spirit is the very life of God. Think what it means for God to give His own Spirit to His child on earth.

Was not this the glory of Jesus as a Son upon earth, that the Spirit of the Father was in Him? At His baptism in Jordan the two things were united: the voice proclaiming Him the beloved Son and the Spirit descending upon Him. And so the apostle says of us, "Because you are sons, God sent the Spirit of his Son into our hearts, the Spirit who calls out, '*Abba*, Father'" (Galatians 4:6). A king seeks in the whole education of his son to develop in him a kingly spirit. Our Father in heaven desires to educate us as His children for the holy, heavenly life in which He dwells. For this He gives us, from the depths of His heart, His own Spirit. This was Jesus' whole aim when, after having made atonement with His own blood, He entered into God's presence to obtain for us, and send down to dwell in us, the Holy Spirit. As the Spirit of the Father and of the Son, the whole life and love of Father and Son are in Him. Coming down into us, He lifts us up into their fellowship. As the Spirit of the Father, He sheds abroad the Father's love with which He loved the Son into our hearts and teaches us to live in that love. As the Spirit of the Son, He breathes into us the childlike liberty, devotion, and obedience in which the Son lived on earth. The Father can bestow no higher or more wonderful gift than this: His own Holy Spirit, the Spirit of sonship.

This truth naturally suggests the thought that this first and best gift of God must be the first and main object of all prayer. For every need of the spiritual life the one thing needful is the Holy Spirit. All the fullness is in Jesus, the fullness of grace and truth out of which we receive grace for grace. The Holy Spirit is the appointed instrument, whose special work it is to make Jesus—and all there is in Him for us—ours in personal appropriation and blessed experience. He is the Spirit of life in Christ Jesus. If we but yield ourselves entirely to the disposal of the Spirit and let Him have His way with us, He will manifest the life of Christ within us. He will do this with divine power, maintaining the life of Christ in us in uninterrupted continuity. Surely if there is one prayer that should draw us to the Father's throne and keep us there, it is for the Holy Spirit, whom we as children have received, to flow into us and out from us in greater fullness.

In the variety of the gifts that the Spirit has to dispense, He meets the believer's every need. Think of the names He bears: He is the Spirit of grace to reveal and impart all the grace there is in Jesus. He is the Spirit of faith, teaching us to begin and go on and increase in believing. He is the Spirit of adoption and assurance, who witnesses that we are God's children and inspires the confident address "Abba, Father!" He is the Spirit of truth to lead into all truth and make each word of God ours in deed and truth. He is the Spirit of prayer, through whom we speak to the Father in prayer that will be heard. He is the Spirit of judgment and burning to search the heart and convict of sin. He is the Spirit of holiness, manifesting and communicating the Father's holy presence within us. He is the Spirit of power, through whom we are strong to testify boldly and work effectively in the Father's service. Lastly, He is the Spirit of glory, the pledge of our inheritance, the preparation and the foretaste of the glory to come. Surely the child of God needs but one thing to be able to live as a child: to be filled with His Spirit.

So Jesus teaches us that the Father is longing to give His Spirit to us if we will but ask in childlike dependence on His promise: "If you ... know how to give good gifts to your children, *how much more* will your Father in heaven give the Holy Spirit to those who ask him!" In God's promise "I will pour out my Spirit *abundantly*," and His command "Be *filled* with the Spirit" (Ephesians 5:18), we see the measure of what God is ready to give and what we may obtain. As God's children we have already received the Spirit, but we still need to pray for His special gifts and enabling as we require them. Not only this, but we also need His unceasing momentary guidance. Just as the branch, even though filled with the sap of the vine, ever cries for the continued and increasing flow of the sap to bring its fruit to perfection, so the believer, rejoicing in the possession of the Spirit, ever thirsts and cries for more. Nothing less than God's promise and God's command should be the measure of our expectation and our prayer. We must be filled abundantly. Ask in the assurance that the wonderful *how much more* of God's Father-love is His pledge that when we ask we receive.

When praying to be filled with the Spirit, do not look for the answer in how you feel. All spiritual blessings must be accepted or taken by faith.[1] The Father *gives* the Holy Spirit

---

[1]The Greek word for receiving and taking is the same. When Jesus said, "Every one that asks *receives*," He used the same verb as at the Supper, "*Take*, eat," and on the Resurrection morning, "*Receive*," accept, take, "the Holy Spirit." Receiving not only implies God's bestowment but also our acceptance.

to His praying child. Even as I pray, I should say in faith, "I have what I ask, the fullness of the Spirit is mine," and then continue steadfast in this faith. On the strength of God's Word we know that we have what we ask. So with thanksgiving that we have been heard, with thanksgiving for what we have received and taken and now hold as ours, let us continue steadfast in believing prayer that the blessing, which has *already* been given us and which we hold in faith, may break through and fill our whole being. In such believing thanksgiving and prayer, our soul opens us up for the Spirit to take entire and undisturbed possession. Such prayer not only asks and hopes but also takes and holds and inherits the full blessing. Remember, if there is one thing on earth we can be sure of, it is this: *The Father desires to have us filled with His Spirit and He delights to give us His Spirit.*

When once we have learned to believe this for ourselves, we may each day take out of the treasury we hold in heaven what liberty and power is needed to pray for the outpouring of the Spirit on the church of God, even on all flesh! He that has once learned to know the Father in prayer learns to pray confidently for others too. The Father gives the Holy Spirit to them that ask Him, especially when we ask for the sake of others.

Father in heaven, you sent your Son to reveal yourself to us, to show us your Father-love. He has taught us that the gift above all gifts that you would give in answer to prayer is the gift of the Holy Spirit.

My Father, I come to you with this prayer: There is nothing I desire so much as to be filled with the Holy Spirit. The blessings He brings are just what I need. He sheds abroad your love in my heart and fills it with yourself. He breathes the mind and life of Christ into me so that I live as He did, in and for the Father's love. He endues with power from on high for all my walk and work. I long for all of this. Father, I beseech you to give me this day the fullness of your Spirit.

I ask for this, resting on the words of my Lord: "How much more . . . the Holy Spirit." I do believe that you hear my prayer and I receive now what I have asked. Father, I claim and take the fullness of your Spirit as mine. I receive the gift this day again as a faith gift. By faith I believe my Father works through the Spirit all He has promised. The Father delights to breathe His Spirit into the waiting child who remains in fellowship with Him. Amen.

Chapter 8

The Boldness of God's Friends

Then he said to them, "Suppose one of you has a friend, and he goes to him at midnight and says, 'Friend, lend me three loaves of bread, because a friend of mine on a journey has come to me, and I have nothing to set before him.' Then the one inside answers, 'Don't bother me. The door is already locked, and my children are with me in bed. I can't get up and give you anything.' I tell you, though he will not get up and give him the bread because he is his friend, yet because of the man's boldness he will get up and give him as much as he needs."

Luke 11:5–8

The first teaching to His disciples was given by our Lord in the Sermon on the Mount. Almost a year later the disciples asked Jesus to teach them to pray. In answer, He gave them the Lord's Prayer a second time, so teaching them *what* to pray. He then speaks of *how* they ought to pray, and repeats what He said before about God's fatherliness and the certainty of an answer. Then He adds the beautiful parable of the friend who came at midnight to teach them the lesson that God wants us to pray not only for ourselves but also for the perishing around us and that in such intercession great boldness is often needed, is always lawful, and even pleasing to God.

The parable is a perfect storehouse of instruction about true intercession. First, there is the *love* that seeks to help the needy: "My friend has come to me." Then the *need* that prompts the cry, "I have nothing to set before him." Then follows the *confidence* that help is to be had: "Suppose one of you has a friend, and says, 'Friend, lend me three loaves of bread.'" An unexpected *refusal* comes: "I *can't* get up and give you anything." But his *perseverance* takes no refusal: "Because of the man's *boldness*..." Last, there comes the reward of such prayer: "He will get up and give him *as much as he needs*." This wonderfully illustrates the way of prayer and faith in which the blessing of God has so often been sought and found.

In the thought of prayer as an appeal to the friendship of God, two lessons are suggested. First, if we are God's friends, and come to Him as such, we must prove ourselves the friends of the needy. God's friendship to us and ours to others go hand in hand. The other lesson is that we may use the utmost liberty in claiming an answer for our needy friends.

So again, prayer has a twofold objective: first, to obtain strength and blessing in our own life; and second, the higher and the true glory of prayer, for which Christ has taken us into His fellowship and teaching, is intercession. In the latter, prayer is the royal power a child of God exercises in heaven on behalf of others and the kingdom. We see in Scripture how in intercession for others Abraham and Moses, Samuel and Elijah, with all the holy men of old, proved that they had power with God and prevailed. When we give ourselves to *be* a blessing, we can count on the blessing of God. When we draw near to God as the friend of the poor and the perishing, we may count on His friendship with us. The righteous man who is the friend of the poor is a special friend of God. This gives wonderful liberty in prayer.

Lord, I have a needy friend whom I must help. As a friend I have undertaken to help him. In you I have a Friend whose kindness and riches I know to be infinite. I am sure you will give me what I ask. If I, being evil, am ready to do for my friend what I can, how much more will you, my heavenly Friend, do for your friend what he asks?

The question may be posed as to whether the fatherhood of God does not give such confidence in prayer that the thought of His friendship can hardly teach us anything more because certainly a father is more than a friend. Still, this pleading the friendship of God opens new wonders to us. That a child obtains what he asks of his father looks so perfectly natural, we almost count it the father's duty to give. But with a friend it seems as if his kindness is more free and dependent, not on nature, but on sympathy and character. Another contrast is that the relationship of a child to his father is more that of perfect dependence, where two friends are nearly on the same level. So our Lord, in unfolding to us the spiritual mystery of prayer, shows His desire to have us approach God in this relationship too—as those whom He has acknowledged as His friends, whose mind and life are in sympathy with His.

But for this we must be *living* as His friends. I am still a child even when a wanderer, but friendship depends upon conduct. "You are my friends if you do what I command" (John 15:14). "You see that his faith and his actions were working together, and his faith was made complete by what he did. And the scripture was fulfilled that says, 'Abraham believed God . . . and he was called *God's friend*' " (James 2:22–23). It is "the *same* Spirit" that leads us that also bears witness to our acceptance with God.

Likewise, also, the same Spirit helps us in prayer. Life as the friend of God gives the wonderful liberty to say, "I have a friend to whom I can go even at midnight." And how much more when I go in the very spirit of that friendship, manifesting myself the very kindness I look for in God, seeking to help my friend as I want God to help me. When I come to God in prayer, He always looks for the motive behind my petition. If it is merely for my own comfort or joy that I seek His grace, I will not receive. But if I can say that it is so that He may be glorified in my passing on His blessing to others, I am not asking in vain. Of course, if I ask for others but wait until God has made me so rich that it will involve no sacrifice or act of faith to help them, I will not receive. But if I can say that I have already undertaken for my needy friend—that in my poverty I have already begun the work of love because I knew I had a friend who would help me—my prayer will be heard. We have no idea how much the plea avails where the friendship of earth looks in its need to the friendship of heaven: "He will . . . give him as much as he needs" (Luke 11:8).

This may not always come all at once. The one thing by which man can honor and enjoy his God is *faith*. Intercession is part of faith's training school. There our friendship with men and with God is tested. Is my friendship with the needy so real that I will take time, sacrifice my rest, and go even at midnight, and not cease until I have obtained for them what I need? Is my friendship with God so clear that I can depend on Him not to turn me away and therefore pray until He gives to me what I ask?

What a deep heavenly mystery there is in persevering prayer. The God who has promised, who longs and whose fixed purpose it is to give the blessing, holds it back. It is to Him a matter of deep importance that His friends on earth should know and fully trust their rich Friend in heaven. For this reason He trains them in the school of "answer delayed" to find out how their perseverance really does prevail and what the mighty power is they can wield in heaven if they but set themselves to it. There is a faith that sees the promise and embraces it and yet does not receive it (Hebrews 11:13, 39). It is when the answer to prayer does not come and the promise we are most firmly trusting appears to be of no effect that the trial of faith more precious than gold takes place. In this trial the faith that has embraced the promise is purified, strengthened, and prepared by personal, holy fellowship with the living God to see His glory. Faith, then, takes and holds the promise until it receives the fulfillment of what was claimed as vital truth from the unseen but living God.

Children of God working in love in your Father's service, take courage. Parents, teachers, preachers—all who have accepted and are bearing the burden of hungry, perishing souls—take courage. That God should truly require persevering prayer, that there should be a spiritual necessity for importunity seems puzzling to us. To teach us, the Master uses this strange parable. If the unfriendliness of a selfish earthly friend can be conquered by importunity, how much more will it avail with our heavenly Friend who loves to give but is held back by our spiritual unfitness and our incapacity to receive what He has to give? Thank Him that by delaying

His answer He is educating us in our true position and the exercise of all our power with Him. He is training us to live with Him in the fellowship of unquestioning faith and trust, to be indeed the friends of God. Let us hold fast the threefold cord that cannot be broken:

1. the hungry friend needing the help;
2. the praying friend seeking the help;
3. the mighty Friend loving to give as much as is needed.

My Blessed Lord and Teacher, I come to you in prayer. Your teaching is so glorious but it is too high for me to grasp. I confess that my heart is too small to comprehend these thoughts of the wonderful boldness I may use with your Father as my Friend. Lord Jesus, I trust you to give me your Spirit and your Word and to make the Word quick and powerful in my heart. I desire to keep this Word: "Because of the man's boldness he will . . . give him as much as he needs" (Luke 11:8).

Lord, teach me to know more of the power of persevering prayer. I see that the Father knows our need of time for the inner life to attain its growth and ripeness so that His grace may indeed be assimilated and made our very own. I know that He wants to train us to exercise a strong faith that does not let Him go even in the face of seeming disappointment. I know He wants to lift us to that wonderful liberty in which we understand how He has made the dispensing of His gift dependent on our prayer. Lord, I say I know this, but teach me to truly understand it in spirit and truth.

Now may it be my joy to act as agent for my rich Friend in heaven and care for all the hungry and perishing—even at midnight. I can do this in confidence because I know my Friend always gives to him who perseveres, because of his importunity, as much as he needs. Amen.

Chapter 9

Prayer Supplies Laborers

*Then he said to his disciples, "The harvest is plentiful but the
workers are few. Ask the Lord of the harvest, therefore,
to send out workers into his harvest field."*

Matthew 9:37–38

The Lord frequently taught His disciples that they must pray,
and how they should pray, but seldom *what* to pray. This He
left to their sense of need and the leading of the Spirit. But
here we have one thing He expressly commands them to
remember. In view of the abundant harvest and the need of
reapers, he tells them to cry to the Lord of the harvest to
send forth laborers. Just as in the parable of the friend at
midnight, He wants them to understand that prayer is not to
be selfish. It is the power through which blessing can come
to others. The Father is Lord of the harvest, so when we pray
for the Holy Spirit, we are to pray that He will prepare and
send out laborers for the work.

Is it not strange that He should ask His disciples to pray
for this? Could He not pray for laborers? Would not one
prayer of His accomplish more than a thousand of theirs?
Did not God, the Lord of the harvest, see the need? Would

He not, in His own good time, send forth laborers—even without the disciples' prayers? Such questions lead us to the deepest mysteries of prayer and its power in the kingdom of God. Answers to such questions convince us that prayer is indeed a power on which the ingathering of the harvest and the coming of the kingdom truly depend.

Prayer is not an empty form or show. The Lord Jesus is Truth. Everything He spoke on earth was truth. "When he saw the crowds, he had compassion on them, because they were harassed and helpless, like sheep without a shepherd" (v. 36). He called on the disciples to pray for laborers to be sent among them. He did so because He really believed that their prayer would effect what was needed. The veil that hides the invisible world from us was transparent to the holy human soul of Jesus. He looked long and deep and far into the hidden connection of cause and effect in the spirit world. He showed from God's Word how, when God called men like Abraham, Moses, Joshua, Samuel, and Daniel, and gave them authority over men in His name, He at the same time gave them the authority and right to call the powers of heaven to their aid as needed. He knew that just as the work of God had been entrusted to these men of old, and to himself for a time here on earth, so now it was about to pass into the hands of His disciples. He knew that when this work was given over to them, it would not be mere form or show. Instead, the success of the work would actually depend on them, whether they were faithful or unfaithful in prayer. As a single individual within the limitations of a human body and a human life, Jesus felt how little a short visit could accomplish among the wandering sheep He saw around Him. He longed for help to have them properly cared for. So He told His disciples to pray—both then and when they would have taken over the work from Him on earth—as one of the chief petitions in their prayer, that the Lord of the harvest himself would send forth laborers into His harvest. The God who entrusted them with the work and made it so largely dependent on them, gives them authority to appeal to Him for laborers to help, and makes the supply dependent on their prayer.

How little Christians feel and intercede for the need of laborers in the fields of the world that are so white for harvest. How little they believe that our labor supply depends on prayer and that prayer will supply as much as is needed (Luke 11:8). It is not that the dearth of labor is not known or discussed, or that efforts are not sometimes put forth to supply the need. But how little the burden of the sheep wandering without a Shepherd is really carried in faith that the Lord of the harvest *would* send forth laborers in answer to prayer. There is no solemn conviction that without this prayer fields ready for reaping will be left to perish. But these are vital truths.

So complete is the surrender of His work into the hands of His church, so dependent has the Lord made himself on them as His body through whom alone His work can be done, and so real is the power that the Lord gives His people to exercise in heaven and on earth, that the number of laborers and the measure of the harvest actually depends upon their prayers.

What a solemn thought! Then why do we not obey the injunction of the Master more wholeheartedly and cry more earnestly for laborers? There are two reasons: First, we lack the compassion of Jesus that gave rise to this request for prayer. When believers learn that the Father's first commandment to His redeemed ones is to love their neighbors as themselves and to live entirely for God's glory, they will accept the care and concern for the perishing as the charge entrusted to them by their Lord. By accepting the lost not only as a field of labor, but as individuals in need of loving care and compassion, the cry will ascend with an earnestness previously unknown: "Lord! Send forth laborers."

The second reason for neglect of the command is a lack of faith. This can be overcome when in true compassion we plead for help. We believe too little in the power of prayer to bring about definite results. We do not live close enough to God and are not given over to His service and kingdom enough to be capable of the confidence that He will give us the faith we need in answer to our prayer. Pray for a life so one with Christ that His compassion will flow into you and His Spirit will give you the assurance that your prayers will be answered.

Such prayer will ask and obtain a double blessing. First there will be the desire for an increase in people entirely given up to the service of God. It is a terrible blot upon the church of Christ that at times individuals simply cannot be found to serve the Master as ministers, missionaries, or teachers of God's Word. As God's children pray for this in their own circle or church, workers will be given. The Lord Jesus is Lord of the harvest. He has been exalted to bestow the gifts of the Spirit. His chief gifts are people filled with the Spirit. But the supply and distribution of these gifts depend on the cooperation of the Head and the body.

The other blessing to be asked is no less important. Every believer is a laborer. Every one of God's children has been redeemed for service and has his work waiting for him. Our prayer should be that the Lord will so fill all His people with a spirit of dedication that not one may be found standing idle in the vineyard. Wherever there is complaint of a lack of workers or of competent helpers for God's work, prayer holds the promise for their supply. There is no work for God where He is not ready and able to provide workers for it. It may take time and importunity, but Christ's command to ask the Lord of the harvest is the pledge that the prayer will be heard: "I tell you, he will get up and give him as much as he needs" (Luke 11:8).

It is a sobering thought that this prayer has been given to us to provide for the world's needs and to obtain helpers for God's work. The Lord of the harvest who told us to pray will hear us. Christ, who called us especially to pray in this way will support our prayers offered in His name and interest. Let us set apart time and give ourselves to this part of our intercessory work. It will lead us into fellowship with His compassionate heart that led Him to call for our prayers in the first place. It will elevate us to an insight into our regal position as those who have had a part with God in the advancement of His kingdom. It will make us feel how truly we are God's fellow workers on earth. A share in His work has been entrusted to us. It will make us partakers not only in the travail but also in the satisfaction of Jesus as we see how blessing has been given in answer to our prayer that otherwise would not have come.

Blessed Lord, you have again given us a wonderful lesson in prayer. We humbly ask you to help us to see clearly the spiritual realities that you speak of. The harvest is so large; the people are perishing. They wait for sleepy disciples to give the signal for laborers to come. Lord, teach us to look upon the harvest with hearts moved with compassion. The laborers are few. Show us how serious is our sin of prayerlessness in this regard.

We know the Lord of the harvest is able and ready to send them forth. Impress on us how important our prayer is—prayer that is sure to be answered.

We do not understand why you trust such work and give such power to people who are so slothful and unfaithful. We thank you for all whom you are teaching to cry day and night for laborers to be sent forth. Breathe your Spirit on all your children that they may learn to live for this alone: the kingdom and glory of their Lord. Make them and us fully awake to faith in what our prayer can accomplish. Fill our hearts with the assurance that prayer offered in loving faith in the living God will bring certain and abundant answer. Amen.

Chapter 10

Prayer Must Be Specific

"What do you want me to do for you?" Jesus asked him.

Mark 10:51

The blind man had been crying out over and over, "Jesus, Son of David, have mercy on me!" The cry reached the ear of the Lord, who knew what the man wanted, and Jesus was ready to give it to him. But first Jesus asks, " 'What do you want me to do for you?' " Jesus wants to hear from the man's own lips not only the general petition for mercy but also the distinct expression of his desire. Until he declares it, he is not healed.

There are still many to whom the Lord puts the same question, and who cannot, until it has been answered, get the help they seek. Our prayers must not be a vague appeal to His mercy or an indefinite cry for blessing, but the distinct expression of a specific need. It is not that Jesus' loving heart does not understand our cry or is not ready to hear, but He desires that we be specific for our own good. Prayer that is specific teaches us to know our own needs better. To find out what our greatest need is demands time, thought, and self-scrutiny. To find out whether our desires are honest and real, and whether we are ready to persevere in them, we are put to the test. It leads us also to discern whether our desires conform to God's Word and whether we really believe that we will receive the things we ask. It helps us to wait for a definite answer and to be aware of it when it comes.

And yet how much of our prayer is vague and pointless. Some cry for mercy without saying why they need mercy. Others ask to be delivered from sin but do not begin by naming any sin from which deliverance may be claimed. Still others pray for God's blessing on those around them, for the outpouring of God's Spirit on their land or the world, and yet do not pinpoint a particular spot where they will wait and expect to see God answer. To all of us, the Lord asks, "What is it you really want and expect me to do?"

Every Christian has only limited powers, and as he must have his own special field of labor in which he works, so his prayers encompass a particular group too. Each believer has his own circle, his family, his friends, and his neighbors. If he were to take one or more of these by name, he would find that this really brings him into the training school of faith and leads to personal and pointed dealing with God. When in such specific matters we have in faith claimed and received answers, then our more general prayers will be believing and effective.

Just as anyone who has hunted wild game knows that firing into the woods does not bring down the target, so in prayer we must have a target, an aim, and then fire upon it directly to see results.

As long as we just pour out our hearts in a multitude of prayer requests without taking time to see whether each one is sent with the purpose and expectation of getting an answer, not many will reach the mark. But if in silence of soul we bow before the Lord and ask ourselves some questions—"What do I really want? Am I asking for it in faith, expecting to receive an answer? Am I ready to place the thing in the Father's keeping and leave it there? Is it settled between God and me that I will receive an answer?"—we will learn to pray in a way that generates faith and expectation and ultimately receives concrete answers.

This is one reason why the Lord warns us against the vain repetitions of the Gentiles, who think they will be heard because they pray so much. We often hear prayers of great earnestness and fervor, in which myriad petitions are poured forth, but to which the Savior would undoubtedly answer, "What do you want me to do for you?"

In a foreign land on business for my father, I would certainly write two different types of letters. There would be family letters, affectionate and newsy, and there would be business letters, containing orders or requests for what I needed sent or done. And there might be letters combining both types of news. The answers would correspond to the letters. To every question and subject of the letters containing the family news, I would not expect a specific answer. But for each business request I made, I would be confident of an answer and expect a desired article would be forwarded to me or a particular request be taken care of at home. This business element must also be present in our dealings with God. Along with our expression of need and sin, of love and faith and consecration, there must be a pointed statement of what we are asking and what we expect to receive. The Father loves to show us His approval and acceptance by His particular answers.

But the word of the Master teaches us more. He is not only saying, "What do you *want*?" but "What do you *will*?"

One often wants something without willing it. I want to have a certain item but I find the price too high, so I resolve not to buy it. I *want* but do not *will* to have it. The sluggard wants to be rich but does not will it. Many a person wants to be saved but is lost because he does not will it. The will rules the whole heart and life. If I really will to have anything that is within my reach, I do not rest until I have it. So when Jesus asks us, "What will you have?" He is asking whether we purpose to have what we ask at any price no matter how great the sacrifice. Do we so will to have our request that even though He delays the answer for a long time we will not rest until He hears and answers us? It is sad that many prayers are merely wishes, sent up for a short time and then forgotten, or sent up year after year as a matter of duty, while we remain content without the answer.

You may ask, "But is it not best to make our wishes known to God and then let Him decide what is best, without seeking to assert our will?" By no means! This is the very essence of the prayer of faith to which Jesus sought to train His disciples: One does not only make known one's desire and then leave the decision to God. That would be a prayer of submission for those cases in which we cannot know God's will. But the prayer of faith, finding God's will in some promise of the Word, pleads for that until it is given. In Matthew 9:28, we read that Jesus asked the blind man, "Do you *believe* that I am able to do this?" Here in Mark 10:51 He asks, "*What do you want* me to do for you?" In both cases He said that faith had saved them (see Matthew 9:29; Mark 10:52). So He said to the Syrophenician woman, "Great is your *faith*! Let it be to you as you *desire*" (Matthew 15:28 NKJV). Faith is nothing but the purpose of the will resting on

God's Word and saying, "I must have this." To believe truly is to will firmly.

But does such a will contradict our dependence on God and our submission to Him? By no means! Rather, it is true submission that honors God. It is only when the child has yielded his own will in entire surrender to the Father that he receives from the Father liberty and power to will what he would have. But when the will of God as revealed through the Word and Spirit has been accepted by the believer as his will too, then the will of God is that His child should use this renewed will in His service. The will is the highest power in the soul. Grace wants above everything to sanctify and restore this will—one of the chief traits of God's image—to full and free exercise. As a son who only lives for his father's will is trusted by the father with his business, so God speaks to His child in all honesty: "What do you want?" Often spiritual sloth under the guise of humility professes to have no will because it fears the trouble of searching out the will of God or the struggle of claiming it in faith when found. True humility is always coupled with strong faith, which only seeks to know the will of God, and then boldly claims fulfillment of the promise "Ask *whatever you wish*, and it will be given you" (John 15:7).

Lord Jesus, teach me to pray with all my heart and strength so clearly that there may be no doubt as to what I have asked. May I know what it is that I desire so that when my petitions are recorded in heaven, I can record them on earth too, and note each answer when it comes. And may my faith in what your Word has promised be so clear that the Spirit may indeed work in me the liberty to will that it come to pass. Lord, renew, strengthen, and sanctify wholly my will for the work of effective prayer.

Blessed Savior, reveal to me the wonderful condescension you show us by asking us to say what it is we want you to do, and promising to do whatever it is we choose. Son of God, I cannot understand it. I can only believe that you have indeed redeemed us wholly for yourself and are seeking to make our will your most efficient servant. Lord, I yield my will unreservedly to you as the power through which your Spirit is to rule my whole being. Let Him take possession of it, lead it into the truth of your promises, and make it so strong in prayer that I may hear you say, "Great is your faith. Be it unto you even as you will." Amen.

Chapter 11

The Faith That Appropriates

Therefore I tell you, whatever you ask for in prayer, believe that you have received it, and it will be yours.

Mark 11:24

What a promise—so large, so divine, that our limited understanding cannot take it in. In every possible way we seek to limit it to what we think safe or probable instead of allowing it just as He gave it in all its quickening power and energy. Faith is very far from being a mere conviction of the truth of God's Word or a conclusion drawn from certain premises. It is the ear that has heard God say what He will do, the eye that has seen Him doing it. Therefore, where there is true faith, the answer *must* come. If we only do the one thing that He asks of us as we pray: "Believe that you have received it," He will do the thing He has promised: "It *will be yours.*" The keynote of Solomon's prayer in 2 Chronicles 6:4, "Praise be to the Lord, the God of Israel, who with his hands has fulfilled what he promised with his mouth to my father David," is the keynote of all true prayer—the joyful adoration of a

God whose hand always secures the fulfillment of what His mouth has spoken. In this spirit let us listen to the promise Jesus gives; each part of it has its divine message.

"Whatever you ask for . . ." At this first phrase our human wisdom at once begins to doubt and ask, "Surely this cannot be literally true?" But if it is not, why did the Master say it and use the strongest expression He could find: "*Whatever* you ask." It is not as if this were the only time He spoke this way—He also said, "*Everything* is possible for him who believes" (Mark 9:23) and "If you have faith . . . *nothing* will be impossible for you" (Matthew 17:20). Faith is so wholly the work of God's Spirit through His Word in the prepared heart of the believing disciple that it is impossible that the fulfillment should not come. Faith is the pledge and forerunner of the coming answer. Yes, "Whatever you ask for in prayer, believe that you have received it." The tendency of human reason is to interpose here certain qualifying clauses—"if expedient," "if according to God's will"—to break the force of a statement that appears presumptuous. Beware of dealing this way with the Master's words. His promise is literally true. He wants His oft-repeated "whatever" to penetrate our hearts and reveal how mighty the power of faith is and how wholly our Father shares His power and places it at the disposal of the child who fully trusts Him. Faith is to have its food and strength in this "whatever"; if we weaken this, we weaken faith. The "whatever" is unconditional. The only condition is what is implied in the believing. Before we can believe, we must determine God's will with certainty. Believing is the exercise of a soul surrendered to the influence of the Word and the Spirit. When once we do believe, nothing will be impossible. God forbid that we should try to bring down His "whatever" to the level of what we think possible. Let us now simply take Christ's Word as the measure and the hope of our faith; it is a seed-word, which, if taken just as He gives it, and kept in the heart, will open and take root, fill our life with its fullness, and bring forth much fruit.

"Whatever you ask for in prayer." Bring whatever you will to God in prayer and receive it from Him. The faith that receives it is the fruit of the prayer. In one aspect there must be faith before there can be prayer; in another, faith is the outcome and the growth of prayer. In the personal presence of the Savior, and fellowship with Him, faith rises to grasp what at first appears too high. In prayer we hold up our desire to the light of God's holy will, our motives are tested, and proof given whether we ask in the name of Jesus and only for the glory of God. In prayer we wait for the leading of the Spirit to show us whether we are asking the right thing in the right spirit. In prayer we become conscious of our lack of faith. We are led on to tell the Father that we do believe, and we prove the reality of our faith by the confidence with which we persevere. In prayer, Jesus teaches and inspires faith. He who hesitates to pray, or who loses heart in prayer because he does not yet feel the faith needed to get the answer, will never learn to believe. He who begins to pray and ask will find the Spirit of faith is given nowhere so surely as at the foot of the throne.

"*Believe* that you have received it." Clearly, what we are to believe is that we receive the very things we ask for. The Savior does not even hint that because the Father knows what is best, He may give us something else. The very mountain that faith bids depart is cast into the sea. There is a prayer in which we make known our requests to God, and the reward is the sweet peace of His keeping our heart and mind at rest. This is the prayer of trust. It has reference to things in which we cannot know the will of God. As children we make known our desires in the countless areas of daily life and leave them to the Father to give or not to give as He sees best. But the prayer of faith that Jesus speaks of is something different, something higher. When in the Master's work or in our daily life the soul sees that nothing so honors the Father as the faith that He will do what He has said—grant us whatever we ask—and then takes its stand on that promise as brought home by the Spirit, it may know for certain that it will receive exactly what it asks. The Lord sets this clearly before us in verse 23: "If anyone . . . does not doubt in his heart, but believes that *what he says* will happen, it will be done for him." This is the blessing of the prayer of faith that Jesus speaks of.

"Believe that you *have received it.*" In this word of central importance, the meaning is too often misunderstood. Believe that you have received the thing you ask for—now, while you are praying. Maybe only later will you have it in personal experience and *see* what you believed; but now, without seeing, you are to believe that it has already been given to you by your Father in heaven. The receiving or accepting of an answer to prayer is just like the receiving or accepting of Jesus or of forgiveness; it is a spiritual thing, an act of faith apart from feeling. When I come to ask for pardon, I believe that Jesus is for me, and so I receive or take Him along with the forgiveness. When I come to ask any special gift according to God's Word, I believe that what I ask for is given to me. I believe that I have it; I hold it in faith. I thank God that it is mine. "And if we know that he hears us—whatever we ask—we know that we have what we have asked of him" (1 John 5:15).

"And it will be yours." That is, the gift that we first held in faith as though already given to us in heaven, will also become ours in personal experience. But will it be necessary to pray longer once we know we have been heard and have received what we asked? Sometimes such prayer will not be necessary, as in cases where the blessing is ready to break through if we but hold on to our confidence and prove our faith by praising Him for what we have received, even though we do not actually have it in experience. In other cases, the faith that has received needs to be still further tried and strengthened in persevering prayer. God alone knows when everything in and around us is fully ripe for the manifestation of the blessing that has been given to faith. Elijah knew for certain that rain would come—God had promised it—and yet he had to pray seven times. But that prayer was not merely show or demonstration; it was an intense spiritual reality in the heart of him who prayed, and in heaven where it had work to do. Through faith *and patience* we inherit the promises. Faith says most confidently, "I have received it." Patience perseveres in prayer until the gift bestowed in heaven is seen on earth. "Believe that you *have received it,* and *it will be yours.*" Between the *have received* in heaven and the *will have* on earth is the link—believing praise and prayer.

Remember, it is Jesus who said these words. As we see heaven opened to us, and the Father on the throne offering to give us whatever we ask in faith, our hearts feel a kind of grief that we have availed ourselves so little of our privilege and that our frail faith still fails to grasp what is so clearly placed within our reach. One fact strengthens our resolve and gives us hope: it is Jesus who has brought us this message from the Father. He himself, when He was on earth, lived the life of faith and prayer. When the disciples expressed surprise at what He did to the fig tree, He told them that the very same faith could be theirs; they could not only command the fig tree but also the mountains, and they must obey. Such faith is intended for us. It is within reach of each one who will but be childlike, yielding to the Father's will and love, trusting the Father's Word and power.

Blessed Lord, you came from the Father to show us all His love and all the treasures of blessing that love is waiting to bestow. You have again flung open the gates wide and given us such promises as to our liberty in prayer that we must blush that we have appropriated so little.

Lord, we look to you to teach us to take and keep and use this precious word of yours: "Whatever you ask for in prayer, believe that you have received." Blessed Jesus, our faith must be rooted in you if it is to grow strong. Your work has freed us from the power of sin and opened the way to the Father. Your love is longing to bring us into the full fellowship of your glory and power. Your Spirit is drawing us upward into a life of faith and confidence. We are convinced that we will learn to pray the prayer of faith. You will train us to pray so that we believe that we truly have what we ask.

Lord, teach me so to know and trust and love you, so to live and abide in you, that my prayers will rise before God in you, and that I may have the full assurance that I am heard. Amen.

Chapter 12

The Secret of Believing Prayer

"Have faith in God," Jesus answered. "I tell you the truth, if anyone says to this mountain, 'Go, throw yourself into the sea,' and does not doubt in his heart but believes that what he says will happen, it will be done for him. Therefore I tell you, whatever you ask for in prayer, believe that you have received it, and it will be yours."

Mark 11:22–24

The promise of answers to prayer is one of the most wonderful lessons in all of Scripture. But in how many hearts has it raised the question "How can I ever attain the faith that knows that it will receive all it asks?" Our Lord answers this question. Before He gave that wonderful promise to His disciples, He told where faith in the answer to prayer begins and always receives its strength. Have faith in God: this word precedes the other where He said to have faith in the promise of an answer to prayer. The power to believe a *promise* depends entirely on faith in *the one who made the promise.* Trust in the person generates trust in his word. Only when we live with God in a personal, loving relationship where God himself is everything to us, only when our whole being is continually opened up and exposed to the mighty working of His holy presence within, is a capacity developed to believe that He gives whatsoever we ask.

This connection between faith in God and faith in His promises becomes clear to us if we think about what faith really is. Often it is compared to the hand or the mouth by which we take and appropriate what is offered to us. But it is important to understand that faith is also the ear by which I hear what is promised, the eye by which I see what is offered to me. On this the power to take depends. I must *hear* the person who gives me the promise. The very tone of his voice gives me courage to believe. I must *see* him. In the light of his eye and countenance, all fear as to my right to take fades away. The value of the promise depends on the one who made the promise. It is on my knowledge of his character that faith in the promise depends. For this reason, before Jesus gives that wonderful prayer-promise, He first says, "Have faith in God." That is, let your eye be open to and gaze on the living God, seeing Him who is invisible. Through the eye I yield myself to the influence of what is before me. I allow it to enter, exert its influence, and leave its impression on my mind. So believing God is simply looking to God and what He is, allowing Him to reveal His presence, giving Him time and yielding the whole being to fully comprehend what He is as God. Believing, the soul opens to receive and rejoice in the overshadowing of His love. Faith is the eye to which God shows what He is and does. Through faith, the light of His presence and the workings of His mighty power stream into the soul. As that which I see lives in me, so by faith God lives in me too.

Faith is also the ear through which the voice of God is heard and intimacy with Him maintained. Through the Holy Spirit the Father speaks to us. The Son is the Word, the substance of what God says. The Spirit is the living voice. The child of God needs this to lead and guide him. The secret voice from heaven must teach him, as it taught Jesus, what to say and what to do. An ear opened toward God, a believing heart waiting on Him to hear what He says, will hear Him speak. The words of God will not only be the words of a book, but because they proceed from the mouth of God, they will be spirit and truth, life and power. They will transform into deed and living experience what are otherwise only thoughts. Through this opened ear the soul waits under the influence of the life and power of God himself. As the words I hear enter my mind and dwell and work there, so through faith God enters my heart to dwell and work there.

When faith is in full exercise as "eye and ear," as the faculty of the soul by which we see and hear God, it will be able to exercise its full power as "hand and mouth," by which we appropriate God and His blessings. The power of *reception* will depend entirely on the power of spiritual *perception*. For this reason, before Jesus gave the promise that God would answer believing prayer, He said, "Have faith in God." Faith is simply surrender. By faith *I yield myself to the living God* because of what I hear and learn about Him. His glory and love fill my heart and master my life. Faith is fellowship. I give myself up to the influence of the friend who has made me a promise, and I become linked to him by it. When we enter into this living fellowship *with God himself* in a faith that always sees and hears Him, it becomes easy and natural to believe His promise as it relates to prayer. Faith in the promise is the fruit of faith in the one who promised. The prayer of faith is rooted in the life of faith. So faith that prays effectively is indeed a gift of God—not as something that He bestows or infuses at once, but in a far deeper and truer sense, as the blessed attitude or habit of soul that grows in us during a life of communion with Him. Surely one who knows his Father well and lives in constant close fellowship with Him finds it a simple thing to believe the promise that the Father will do the will of His child.

It is because many of God's children do not understand this connection between the life of faith and the prayer of faith that their experience of the power of prayer is so limited. When they earnestly desire to obtain an answer from God, they fix their whole heart upon the promise and try their utmost to grasp it in faith. When they do not succeed, they give up hope. The promise is true, but it is beyond their power to take hold of it in faith.

Jesus taught: Have faith in God, the living God. Let faith look to God more than toward the thing promised. God's love, power, and His living presence will awaken and build up faith.

To someone asking for some means to get more strength in his arms and hands to be able to seize and hang on to things, a physician would say that his whole constitution must be built up and strengthened. So the cure of a weak faith is only found by revitalizing our whole spiritual life through close fellowship with God. Learn to believe in God, take hold of God, let God take possession of your life, and it will be easy to take hold of the promises. He who knows and trusts God will find it easy to trust the promises too.

This is demonstrated clearly in the saints of old. Every special exhibition of the power of faith was the fruit of a special revelation of God. See it in Abraham: *"The word of the Lord came to Abram in a vision: 'Do not be afraid, Abram. I am your shield, your very great reward'. . . . He took him outside and said . . . Abram believed the Lord"* (Genesis 15:1, 5–6). Later *"The Lord appeared to him and said, 'I am God Almighty'. . . . Abram fell facedown, and God said to him, 'As for me, this is my covenant with you'"* (Genesis 17:1, 3–4). The revelation of God himself gave the promise its living power to enter the heart and build faith. Because they knew God, these men of faith trusted His promise. God's promise will be to us what God himself is. The man who walks before the Lord and falls upon his face to listen while the living God speaks to him will be the one who will receive the promise.

Though we have God's promises in the Bible, and full liberty to receive them, spiritual power will be lacking unless God himself speaks them to us. And He speaks to those who walk and live with Him. Therefore, have faith in God: Let faith be "eyes and ears," then surrender to let God reveal himself fully in the soul. Count it one of the chief blessings of prayer to exercise faith in God as the living, mighty God who waits to fulfill in us all the good pleasure of His will and the work of faith with power. See Him as the God of love, whose delight is to bless and impart himself to us. In such worship of faith in God, the power will speedily grow to believe His promise: "If you believe, you will receive whatever you ask for in prayer" (Matthew 21:22). In faith make God your own; then the promise will be yours also.

Jesus teaches us that although we seek God's gifts, God wants to give us himself first. We think of prayer as the power to draw good gifts from heaven and Jesus as the means to draw ourselves up to God. We want to stand at the door and cry, but Jesus would have us first enter in and realize that we are His friends and children. Let us accept the teaching; let every experience of the smallness of our faith in prayer urge us to have and exercise more faith in the living God, and then in such faith to yield ourselves to Him. A heart full of God has power for the prayer of faith. Faith in God begets faith in the promise of an answer to prayer.

Therefore, child of God, take time to bow before Him and to wait on Him to reveal himself. Take time to let your soul in holy awe and worship exercise and express its faith in the Infinite One. As He imparts himself and takes possession of you, the prayer of faith will crown your faith in God.

0 my God, I do believe in you. I believe in you as the Father, infinite in your love and power; and as the Son, my Redeemer and my life; and as the Holy Spirit, Comforter and Guide and strength. Three-in-One God, I have faith in you. I know and am assured that all you are, you are to me, that all you have promised you will perform.

Lord Jesus, increase my faith. Teach me to take time to wait and worship in your holy presence until my faith takes in all there is in my God for me. Let it see Him as the fountain of all life, working with almighty strength to accomplish His will in the world and in me. Let it see Him in His love longing to meet and fulfill my desires. Let it so take possession of my heart and life that through faith God alone may dwell there. Lord Jesus, help me! With my whole heart I want to believe in God.

Blessed Savior, how can your church glorify you? How can it fulfill that work of intercession through which your kingdom must come unless our whole life is faith in God? Speak that word into the depths of our souls. Amen.

Chapter 13

The Cure of Unbelief

Then the disciples came to Jesus privately and said, "Why
could we not cast it out?" So Jesus said to them, "Because of
your unbelief; for assuredly, I say to you, if you have faith
as a mustard seed . . . nothing will be impossible for you.
However, this kind does not go out except
by prayer and fasting."

Matthew 17:19–21 NKJV

When the disciples saw Jesus cast the evil spirit out of the
epileptic whom they could not cure, they asked the Master
for the cause of their failure. He had given them power and
authority over all demons, and the power to cure all diseases.
They had often exercised that power and joyfully told how
the demons were subject to them. But now, while He was on
the Mount, they had utterly failed. It had been proven that
there was nothing in the will of God or in the nature of the
case to render deliverance impossible. At Christ's bidding,
the evil spirit had left the man.

From their question, "Why could we not cast it out?" it
is evident that they had tried to do so. They had probably
used the Master's name and called upon the evil spirit to

leave. But their efforts had been in vain, and in the presence of the multitude they had been put to shame.

Christ's answer was plain: "Because of your unbelief." The cause of His success and their failure was not due to His having a special power to which they had no access. No, the reason was not so hard to find. He had often taught them that there is one power—faith—to which in the kingdom of darkness, as well as in the kingdom of God, everything must bow. In the spiritual world failure has but one cause: the lack of faith.

Faith is the one condition on which all divine power can enter into man and work through him. It is the acceptance of the unseen: man's will yielded up to and molded by the will of God. The power they had received to cast out demons, they did not hold in themselves as a permanent gift or possession. The power was in Christ, to be received and held and used by a living faith in Him alone. Had they been full of faith in Him as Lord and conqueror in the spirit world, had they been full of faith in Him as having given them authority to cast out demons in His name, this faith would have given them the victory. "Because of your unbelief" has been for all time the Master's explanation and reproof of failure in His church.

But lack of faith must have a cause. The disciples might well have asked: "And why could we not believe? Our faith has cast out demons before. Why have we failed now in believing?" The Master proceeds to tell them before they ask: "This kind does not go out except by prayer and fasting."

As faith is the simplest, so it is the highest exercise of the spiritual life, where our spirit yields itself in perfect receptivity to God's Spirit and so is strengthened to its highest activity. This faith depends entirely upon the state of our spiritual life. Only when this is strong and in full health, when the Spirit of God has full sway in our life, is there the power of faith to do its work.

The faith that can overcome such stubborn resistance as you have just seen in this evil spirit, Jesus tells them, is not possible except to men living in very close fellowship with God and in special separation from the world—in prayer and fasting. And so He teaches two lessons of deep importance about prayer. First, faith needs a life of prayer in which to grow and remain strong. Second, prayer sometimes needs to be combined with fasting for its perfect development.

Faith needs a life of prayer in which to grow and remain strong. In all the various parts of the spiritual life, there is such close union, such unceasing action and reaction, that each may be both cause and effect. This is also true with faith. There can be no true prayer without faith. Some measure of faith must precede prayer. Prayer is also the way to more faith. There can be no higher degrees of faith except through much prayer. This is the lesson Jesus teaches here.

Nothing needs to grow as much as our faith. "Your faith is growing more and more" is said of one church (2 Thessalonians 1:3). When Jesus said, "According to your faith will it be done to you" (Matthew 9:29), He announced the law of the kingdom, which tells us that all do not have equal degrees of faith, that the same person does not always have the same degree, and that the measure of faith determines the measure of power and blessing. If we want to know where and how our faith is to grow, the Master points us to the throne of God. In prayer, in the exercise of the faith I have, in fellowship with the living God, faith can increase. Faith can live only by feeding on what is divine: God himself.

It is in the adoring worship of God, the waiting on Him

and for Him, the deep silence of soul that yields to God to reveal himself, that the capacity for knowing and trusting God will be developed. As we read His Word, let us ask Him to open it to us and make it His own personal, living word to our hearts. It is in prayer, in living contact with God, that faith—the power to trust God and accept everything He says—will become strong in us.

Many Christians do not understand what is meant by the often spoken of "much prayer." They cannot conceive of spending extended time with God. But what the Master says and what the experience of His people has confirmed is that people of strong faith are people of much prayer.

This brings us again to Jesus' first lesson, "Have faith in God" (Mark 11:22). Our faith must strike its roots deep and broad into the living God; then that faith will be strong to remove mountains and cast out demons. "If you have faith . . . nothing will be impossible for you."

If we give ourselves to the work God has for us in the world—coming into contact with the mountains and the demons there are to be cast away and cast out—we will soon comprehend the need there is of much faith, and of much prayer as the only soil in which faith can be cultivated.

Christ Jesus is our life and the life of our faith. It is His life in us that makes us strong and makes it easy to believe. In the dying to self that much prayer implies, in closer union to Jesus, the spirit of faith will come in power. *Faith needs prayer* for its full growth.

Sometimes prayer needs to be combined with fasting for its perfect development. This is the second lesson. Prayer is like one hand grasping the invisible; fasting is like the other letting go of the visible. In nothing is man more closely connected with the world of sense than in his need of food and his enjoyment of it. It was the fruit, good for food, with which man was tempted and fell in Paradise. When Jesus was hungry in the wilderness, it was with bread to be made from stones that He was tempted, and in fasting that He triumphed. The body has been redeemed to be a temple of the Holy Spirit; it is in body as well as spirit, Scripture says, in eating and drinking, we are to glorify God. There are many Christians to whom this eating to the glory of God has not yet become a spiritual reality. The first thought suggested by Jesus' words about fasting and prayer is that only in a life of moderation and temperance and self-denial will there be the heart or the strength to pray much.

But there is also a more literal meaning. Sorrow and anxiety cannot eat. Joy celebrates in feasts with eating and drinking. There may come times of eating and drinking. There may come times when it is strongly felt that the body and its appetites—as legitimate as they are—hinder the spirit in its battle with the powers of darkness, and at such times it will be necessary to refrain from eating. We are creatures of the senses. Our mind is helped by what comes to us embodied in concrete form. Fasting helps to express, to deepen, and to confirm, the resolution that we are ready to sacrifice anything to attain what we seek for the kingdom of God. He who accepted the fasting and sacrifice of the Son values and accepts and rewards with spiritual power the soul that is ready to give up all for Christ and His kingdom.

So prayer is reaching out after God and the unseen; fasting is letting go of all that is of the seen and temporal. Ordinary Christians imagine that all that is not positively forbidden and sinful is lawful to them, and they seek to retain as much as possible of this world, its properties, its literature, and its enjoyments. In contrast, the truly consecrated soul is like the soldier who carries only what he needs for battle. Laying aside every weight and the sin that easily trips up, afraid of entangling himself with the affairs of this life, he seeks to lead a life as one especially set apart for the Lord and His service. Without such voluntary separation—even from what is lawful—no one will attain full power in prayer.

Disciples of Jesus who have asked the Master to teach you to pray, come now and accept His lessons. He tells you that prayer is a path to faith, strong faith that can cast out demons. He tells you, "If you have faith . . . nothing will be impossible for you" (Matthew 17:20). Let this glorious promise encourage you to pray much. Is not the prize worth the price? Should we not give up all to follow Jesus in the path He opens to us here? Should we not, if need be, fast? Should we not do anything in the body or in the world around us that hinders our life work: having an intimate relationship with our God in prayer and becoming people of faith whom He can use in His work of saving the world.

Lord Jesus, how continually you must reprove us for our unbelief! How strange it must appear to you, our recurring incapacity for trusting our Father and His promises. Lord, let your reproof, with its searching "Because of your unbelief," sink into the very depths of our hearts and reveal to us how much of sin and suffering around us is because of our lack of believing prayer. Then teach us, Lord, that there is a place where faith can be learned and obtained: the place of prayer and fasting, bringing us into living and abiding fellowship with you and the Father.

You are the author and perfecter of our faith. Teach us to allow you to live in us by your Holy Spirit. Our efforts and prayers for grace to believe have been so unavailing. We have looked for strength in ourselves that can only be given by you. Show us that our faith grows in the place of prayer, in the ministry of intercession, and in fasting. Amen.

Chapter 14

Prayer and Love

And when you stand praying, if you hold anything against
anyone, forgive him, so that your Father in heaven
may forgive you your sins.

Mark 11:25

These words follow the promise "If you believe, you will
receive whatever you ask for in prayer" (Matthew 21:22).
Before that, "Have faith in God" (Mark 11:22) taught us that
effective prayer depends upon our clear relationship to God.
Now these words remind us that our relationship with our
fellowmen must be clear too. Love to God and love to our
neighbor are inseparable. Prayer from a heart that is not
right—either with God or with others—cannot prevail. Faith
and love are essential to each other.

Our Lord frequently emphasized this thought. When
speaking about the sixth commandment, He taught His disciples that acceptable worship of the Father was impossible if
everything was not right with our fellowman. "If you are
offering your gift at the altar and there remember that your
brother has something against you, leave your gift there in
front of the altar. First go and be reconciled to your brother;

then come and offer your gift" (Matthew 5:23–24). Later He taught us to pray, "Forgive us our debts, as we also have forgiven our debtors" (Matthew 6:12). Then at the close of the prayer, He added, "If you do not forgive men their sins, your Father will not forgive your sins" (Matthew 6:15). At the close of the parable of the unmerciful servant, He applies His teaching: "This is how my heavenly Father will treat each of you unless you forgive your brother from your heart" (Matthew 18:35).

Now beside the dried-up fig tree, He speaks of the wonderful power of faith and the prayer of faith. All at once—apparently without connection—He introduces the thought "And when you stand praying, if you hold anything against anyone, forgive him, so that your Father in heaven may forgive you your sins" (Mark 11:25). Throughout His life in Nazareth and afterward, the Lord learned that disobedience to the law of love was a common sin even among praying people, and a cause of the weakness of their prayer. He now wants to lead us into His own blessed experience that nothing gives such liberty of access and such power in believing as the consciousness that we have given ourselves in love and compassion for those whom God loves.

The first lesson taught here is that of a forgiving disposition. We pray, "Forgive, *even as* we have forgiven." Scripture says, "Forgive each other, just as in Christ God forgave you" (Ephesians 4:32). God's full and free forgiveness is to be our rule with others. Otherwise, our reluctant, halfhearted forgiveness, which is not forgiveness at all, will be God's rule with us. Every prayer rests upon our faith in God's pardoning grace. If God dealt with us according to our sins, not one prayer would be heard.

Pardon opens the door to all God's love and blessing.

Because God has forgiven our sins, our prayer can prevail to obtain what we need. The deep, sure ground of answers to prayer is God's forgiving love. When it possesses our heart, we pray in faith and we live in love. God's forgiving disposition, revealed in His love to us, becomes our disposition as well. As the power of His forgiving love penetrates our heart and dwells within us, we forgive as He forgives. If there is any great injury or injustice done to us, we first try to possess a Christlike disposition; to be kept from a sense of wounded honor, from a desire to maintain our rights, or from rewarding the offender as he deserves.

In the little annoyances of daily life, we are careful not to excuse the hasty temper, the sharp word, and the quick judgment, rationalizing that we mean no harm, that we do not stay angry for long, or that it would be too much to expect from weak human nature that we should forgive as God does. No, we take the command literally: "*Even as* Christ forgave you, so you *also* must do" (Colossians 3:13 NKJV). The blood that cleanses the conscience from dead works cleanses from selfishness too. The love it reveals is pardoning love that takes possession of us and flows through us to others. Our forgiving love to men is the evidence of the reality of God's forgiving love in us, and so it is a condition for the prayer of faith.

There is a second, more general lesson: Our daily life in the world is the test of our relationship with God in prayer. How often the Christian, when he goes to pray, does his utmost to cultivate certain frames of mind that he thinks will be pleasing. He does not understand, or forgets, that life does not consist of so many loose pieces, of which first one and then another can be taken up. Life is a whole. Our frame of mind in the hour of prayer is judged by God against the total frame of mind of our ordinary daily life of which that hour is but a small part. Not the feeling I muster up in prayer but the tone of my life during the day is God's criterion of what I really am and desire. My drawing near to God is one with my relationship with others; failure here will cause failure there. Not only the distinct consciousness of anything wrong between my neighbor and myself, but also the ordinary current of my thinking and judging, or unloving thoughts and words I allow to pass unnoticed, can hinder my prayer. The effective prayer of faith comes from a life surrendered to the will and the love of God. My prayer is measured not according to what I try to be when I am praying but by what I am when I am not praying.

These thoughts form a third lesson. In our life with others, the one thing on which everything depends is love. The spirit of forgiveness is the spirit of love. Because God is love, He forgives. Only when we are dwelling in love can we forgive as God forgives. In love for the brethren we have the evidence of love for the Father, the ground of confidence before God, and the assurance that our prayer will be heard.

Let us love in deed and truth; *hereby* shall we assure our heart before Him. If our heart does not condemn us, we have boldness toward God, and whatever we ask we receive of Him. Neither faith nor work will profit if we have not love. It is love that unites us with God. Love proves the reality of faith. As essential as the word in Mark 11:22, "Have faith in God," is the one that follows it in verse 25: "If you hold anything against anyone, forgive him." Right relations, both with God and with those around me, are conditions of effective prayer.

This love is of special consequence when we pray for others. We sometimes work for Christ out of zeal for His cause or for our own spiritual health without giving ourselves in self-sacrificing love for those whose souls we seek. No wonder our faith is weak and does not accomplish what we wish.

To look on a soul, no matter how unlovable, in the light of the tender love of Jesus the Shepherd seeking the lost; to see Jesus Christ in that one, and for Jesus' sake to take him up in prayer with a heart that truly loves—this is the secret of believing prayer and of results. In speaking of forgiveness, Jesus speaks of love as its root. In the Sermon on the Mount, He connected His teaching and promises about prayer with the call to be merciful as the Father in heaven is merciful (Matthew 5:7, 9, 22, 38–48), and again, here we see that a loving life is the condition of believing prayer.

Nothing is so heart-searching as believing prayer, or even the honest effort to pray in faith. Let us not dull the edge of that self-examination by the thought that God does not hear our prayer for reasons known to Him alone. "When you ask, you do not receive, because you ask with wrong motives" (James 4:3). Let that word of God search us.

Is our prayer the true expression of a life wholly given over to the will of God and the love of man? Love is the only soil in which faith can put down roots and thrive. As it throws its arms up and opens its heart heavenward, the Father always looks to see if it has them opened toward the evil and the unworthy too. In that love—not of perfect attainment but the love of fixed purpose and sincere obedience—faith alone can obtain the blessing. He who gives himself to allow the love of God to dwell in him, and in the practice of daily life to love as God loves, will have the power to believe in the Love that hears his every prayer. It is *the Lamb* who is in the midst of the throne; it is suffering and forbearing love that prevails with God in prayer. The merciful shall obtain mercy. The meek shall inherit the earth.

Blessed Father, you are Love, and only he who abides in love abides in you and in fellowship with you. The blessed Son has again taught me how deeply true this is in my fellowship with you in prayer. O God, let your love, planted in my heart by the Holy Spirit, be in me a fountain of love to all those around me, that out of my life may spring the power of believing prayer. Especially help me to find in the joy with which I forgive day by day whoever might offend me, the proof that your forgiveness is power and life.

Lord Jesus, my blessed teacher, teach me to forgive. Let the power of your blood make the pardon of my sins such a reality that forgiveness, as shown by you to me, and by me to others, may be the very joy of heaven. Show me whatever in my relationship with others might hinder my fellowship with you, so that my daily life in my own home and in society may be the school in which strength and confidence are gathered for the prayer of faith. Amen.

Chapter 15

The Power of United Prayer

*Again, I tell you that if two of you on earth agree about
anything you ask for, it will be done for you by my Father in
heaven. For where two or three come together in
my name, there am I with them.*

Matthew 18:19–20

One of the first lessons our Lord taught about prayer was
that the pray-er was not to be seen of men. Enter an inner
room and get alone with the Father. A second lesson would
be that we need not only secret and solitary prayer but also
public, united prayer. He gives a very special promise for the
united prayer of two or three who agree in what they ask.
For its full development, a tree has its root hidden in the
ground and its stem growing up into the sunlight. In the
same way prayer equally needs both the hidden secrecy in
which the soul meets God alone and the public fellowship
with those who find in the name of Jesus their common
meeting place.

The reason for this is plain. The bond that unites a

Christian to his fellowman is no less real and close than that which unites him to God: He is one with them. Grace renews our relationship not only to God but also to man. We learn to say not only "*My* Father" but "*Our* Father." Nothing would be more unnatural than for each child of a family to always meet with his father separately but never in the united expression of the family's desires or love. Believers are members not only of one family but also of one body. Just as each member of the body depends on the others, and the full action of the spirit dwelling in the body depends on the union and cooperation of all, so Christians cannot reach the full blessing God is ready to give through His Spirit unless they seek and receive it in fellowship with one another. In the union and fellowship of believers, the Spirit is free to manifest His full power. It was to the one hundred twenty continuing in one place together, and praying with one accord, that the Spirit of the glorified Lord came down.

The marks of true united prayer are given to us in these words of our Lord: the first is *agreement* as to the thing asked. There must be not only a general consent to agree with anything another may ask but also some special matter of distinct united desire; as in all prayer, the agreement must be in spirit and in truth. In such agreement it will become very clear to us exactly what we are asking and whether we may confidently ask according to God's will; also whether we are ready to believe that we have received what we ask.

The second mark concerns the *gathering together in the name of Jesus.* Later we shall learn much more of the need and the power of the name of Jesus in prayer; here our Lord teaches us that the name must be the center of the union for believers, the bond that unites them into one, just as a home contains and unites all who are in it.

"The name of the Lord is a strong tower; the righteous run to it and are safe" (Proverbs 18:10). That name is a reality to those who understand and believe in it; to meet in it is to have the Lord himself present. The love and unity of His disciples attract Jesus. "For where two or three come together in my name, *there am I with them*" (Matthew 18:20). The living presence of Jesus in the fellowship of His loving, praying disciples gives united prayer its power.

The third mark is the certain answer: "It will be done for you by my Father" (Matthew 18:19). A prayer meeting for maintaining Christian fellowship or seeking our own edification may have its use; but this was not the Savior's view in its appointment. He meant it as a means of securing *special answers to prayer*. A prayer meeting without recognized answers to prayer ought to be an anomaly. When any of us has distinct desires for which we lack sufficient faith to believe for answers, we ought to seek strength in the help of others. In the unity of faith, of love, and of the Spirit, the power of the name and the presence of Jesus is more free to act and the answer comes more surely. The evidence that there has been true united prayer is the answer or the receiving of the thing we have asked, "I tell you . . . *it will be done for you by my Father in heaven*" (Matthew 18:19).

What an unspeakable privilege united prayer is and what a power it can be . . .

1. if the believing husband and wife knew that they were joined together in the name of Jesus to experience His presence and power in united prayer (1 Peter 3:1–8);
2. if friends believed what mighty help two or three praying together could give each other;
3. if in every prayer meeting the coming together in His name, faith in His presence, and the expectation of the

answer were of foremost importance;

4. if in every church united, effective prayer were regarded as one of the chief purposes for which they are banded together and the highest exercise of their power as a church;

5. if in the church universal the coming of the kingdom, the coming of the King himself—first in the mighty outpouring of His Holy Spirit, and then in His own glorious person—were really matters of unceasing, united crying to God.

Who can say what blessing might come to and through those who agree in this way to prove God in the fulfillment of His promise?

In the apostle Paul we see very distinctly what a reality his faith in the power of united prayer was. To the Romans he writes, "I urge you, brothers, by our Lord Jesus Christ and by the love of the Spirit, to *join me in my struggle* by praying to God for me" (Romans 15:30). In answer, he expects to be delivered from his enemies and to be prospered in his work.

To the Corinthians, "[God] will continue to deliver us, as you help us by your prayers" (2 Corinthians 1:11), their prayer is to have a real share in his deliverance.

To the Ephesians, he writes, "And pray in the Spirit on all occasions . . . for all the saints. Pray also for me, that whenever I open my mouth, words may be given me" (Ephesians 6:18–19). His power and success in his ministry depend on their prayers.

With the Philippians, he expects that his trials will turn to his salvation and the progress of the gospel "*through your prayers* and the help given by the Spirit of Jesus Christ" (Philippians 1:19).

To the Colossians, he adds to the injunction to continue

steadfast in prayer: "And pray for us, too, that God may open a door for our message" (Colossians 4:3).

And to the Thessalonians, he writes, "Finally, brothers, pray for us that the message of the Lord may spread rapidly and be honored. . . . And pray that we may be delivered from wicked and evil men" (2 Thessalonians 3:1).

Everywhere it is evident that Paul felt himself to be the member of a body on whose sympathy and cooperation he was dependent. He counted on the prayers of these churches to obtain for him what otherwise might not be given. The prayers of the church were to him as real a factor in the work of the kingdom as the power of God.

Who can say what power a church could develop and exercise if it gave itself to the work of prayer day and night for the coming of the kingdom, for God's power on His servants and His Word, for the glorifying of God in the salvation of souls?

Most churches think their members are gathered into one simply to take care of and build each other up. They do not know that God rules the world by the prayers of His saints; that prayer is the power by which Satan is conquered; that by prayer the church on earth has at its disposal the powers of the heavenly world. They do not remember that by His promise Jesus has consecrated every assembly in His name to be a gate of heaven where His presence is to be felt and His power experienced in the Father's fulfilling of their desires.

We cannot sufficiently thank God for any occasion of united prayer with which Christians cooperate and engage themselves. It is of unspeakable value as proof of their unity and faith in the power of united prayer. It trains them to enlarge their hearts to take in all the needs of the church universal and continue in persevering prayer. But especially as a stimulus to continued union in prayer in the smaller circles, its blessing has been great. It will become even greater as God's people recognize what it is for all to meet as one in the name of Jesus, as they have His presence in the midst of a body united in the Holy Spirit, boldly claiming the promise that what they agree to ask shall be done by the Father.

Blessed Lord, in your high-priestly prayer you asked earnestly for the unity of your people. Now teach us how you invite and urge us to this unity by your precious promise concerning united prayer. When we are one in love and desire, our faith has your presence and the Father's answer.

Father, we pray for your people, and for every smaller circle of those who meet together, that they may be one. Remove all selfishness and self-interest, all narrow-mindedness and estrangement that hinder such unity. Cast out the spirit of the world and the flesh through which your promise loses all its power. Let the thought of your presence and the Father's favor draw us all nearer to one another.

Grant especially, blessed Lord, that your church may come to believe that by the power of united prayer she can bind and loose in heaven, that Satan can be cast out, that souls can be saved, that mountains can be removed, and that the kingdom can be hastened to come. And grant, Lord, that in the circle with which I pray, the prayer of the church may indeed be the power through which your name and your Word are glorified. Amen.

Chapter 16

The Power of Persevering Prayer

Then Jesus told his disciples a parable to show them that they should always pray and not give up. . . . And the Lord said, "Listen to what the unjust judge says. And will not God bring about justice for his chosen ones, who cry out to him day and night? Will he keep putting them off?" I tell you, he will see that they get justice, and quickly.

Luke 18:1, 6–8

Of all the mysteries of the prayer world, the need of persevering prayer is one of the greatest. We cannot easily understand that the Lord, who is so loving and longing to bless, should have to be asked time after time, sometimes year after year, before the answer comes. This is also one of the greatest practical difficulties in the exercise of believing prayer. After persevering supplication, when your prayer remains unanswered, it is often easiest for our slothful flesh—with the appearance of pious submission—to think that we must now cease praying because God may have His secret reason for withholding His answer to our request.

By faith alone the difficulty is overcome. When once faith has taken its stand upon God's Word and the name of Jesus, and has yielded itself to the leading of the Spirit to seek only God's will and honor in its prayer, it need not be discouraged by delay. It knows from Scripture that the power of believing prayer is simply irresistible. Real faith can never be disappointed.

To exercise the irresistible power it can have, faith, just like water, must be gathered up and accumulated until the stream can come down in full force. Often there must be a heaping up of prayer until God sees that the measure is full—and then the answer comes. Just as the plowman has to take his ten thousand steps and sow his ten thousand seeds, each one a part of the preparation for the final harvest, so there is a need for oft-repeated persevering prayer, all working out some desired blessing. It knows for certain that not a single believing prayer can fail of its effect in heaven, but each has its influence and is treasured up to work toward an answer in due time to the one who perseveres to the end.

Faith knows that it deals not with human thoughts or possibilities but with the Word of the living God. Just as Abraham through so many years "in hope believed against hope" (Romans 4:18 NASB), and then "through faith *and patience* inherited the promise" (Hebrews 6:12), faith believes that the long-suffering of the Lord is salvation, *waiting for* the coming of its Lord to fulfill His promise.

To enable us to combine quiet patience and joyful confidence in our persevering prayer when the answer to our prayer does not come at once, we particularly need to understand the two words by which our Lord describes the character and conduct not of the unjust judge but of our God and Father toward those whom He allows to cry day and night to Him: "Will he keep *putting them off*? . . . He will see that they get justice, and *quickly*" (Luke 18:7–8).

He will avenge them *quickly*, the Master says. The blessing is all prepared. He is not only willing but anxious to give them what they ask. Everlasting love burns with the longing desire to reveal itself fully and satisfy the needs of its beloved. God will not delay one moment longer than is absolutely necessary. He will do all in His power to hasten and speed the answer.

But if this is true and His power is infinite, why does the answer to prayer often delay so long? Why must God's own elect, so often in the midst of suffering and conflict, cry day and night?

"Will he keep *putting them off*?" (Luke 18:7). "See how the farmer waits for the land to yield its valuable crop and how patient he is for autumn and spring rains" (James 5:7). The farmer does indeed long for his harvest, but knows that it must have its full time of sunshine and rain, and so has much patience. A child so often wants to pick the half-ripe fruit; the farmer knows to wait until the proper time. Man, in his spiritual nature, too, is under the law of gradual growth that reigns in all created life. Only in the path of development can he reach his divine destiny. And it is the Father, in whose hands are the times and seasons, who alone knows the moment when the soul or the church is ripened to that fullness of faith in which it can receive and maintain the blessing. As a father longs to have his only child home from school but waits patiently until the time of training is completed, so it is with God and His children. He is the long-suffering One and answers speedily (at the right time).

Insight into this truth leads the believer to cultivate corresponding attitudes. *Patience* and *faith*, *waiting* and *hastening*, are the secrets of his perseverance. By faith in God's promise, we know that we *have* the petitions we have asked of Him. Faith takes hold of the answer in the promise as an unseen spiritual possession and then rejoices and praises God for it.

But there is a difference between the faith that holds the Word and knows it has the answer, and the clearer, fuller, riper faith that claims the promise as a present experience. It is in persevering, not unbelieving, but confident and praiseful prayer, that the soul grows up into that full union with its Lord in which it can enter upon the possession of the blessing in Him. Before the answer can fully come there may be things that have to be put right—in those around us, in humankind as a whole, or in God's government—but the faith that has according to the Word believed that it has received can allow God to take His time. It knows it has prevailed and must prevail. In quiet, persistent, and determined perseverance, it continues in prayer and thanksgiving until the blessing comes. So we see combined what at first sight appears contradictory: faith that rejoices in the answer from the unseen God as a present possession, along with the patience that cries day and night until it is revealed. The *quickly* of God's *putting them off* is met by the triumphant but patient faith of His waiting child.

The great danger in this school of delayed answers is the temptation to think that it may not be God's will after all to give us what we ask. If our prayer is according to God's Word and after the leading of the Spirit, let us not give way to these fears. Let us learn to give God time. God needs time with us. If we only give Him time—in daily fellowship with Him—for Him to exercise the full influence of His presence on us, and time—day by day, in the course of our being kept waiting—for faith to prove its reality and to fill our whole being, then He will lead us from faith to vision. We will see the glory of God.

Let no delay shake our faith. Faith also yields—first the blade, then the ear, then the full corn in the ear. Each believing prayer brings the final victory a step nearer. Each believing prayer helps to ripen the fruit and bring it closer; fills up the measure of prayer and faith known to God alone; conquers the hindrances in the unseen world; hastens the end. Child of God, give the Father time. He is long-suffering over you. He wants the blessing to be rich and full and sure. Give Him time, while you cry day and night. Only remember the word: "I tell you, he will see that they get justice, and quickly" (Luke 18:8).

The blessing of such persevering prayer is unspeakable. Nothing is so heart-searching as the prayer of faith. It teaches you to discover and confess and give up everything that hinders the coming of the blessing and everything that may not be in accordance with the Father's will. It creates a closer fellowship with Him who alone can teach us to pray. It leads to a more entire surrender, to draw near under no covering but that of the blood and the Spirit. It calls to a closer and simpler abiding in Christ alone. Christian, give God time. He will perfect that which concerns you. "Putting them off—quickly" is God's watchword as you enter the gates of prayer. Let it be yours too.

Let it be this way whether you pray for yourself or for others. All labor, bodily or mental, needs time and effort. We must give *ourselves* to it. Nature reveals her secrets and yields her treasures only to diligent and thoughtful labor. However little we can understand it, in spiritual husbandry it is the same: the seed we sow in the soil of heaven, the efforts we put forth and the influence we seek to exert in the world above, need our whole being—we must give ourselves to prayer. But let us hold fast the confidence that in due season we shall reap if we faint not.

Remember this lesson as we pray for the church of Christ. She is indeed like the poor widow who, in the absence of her Lord is apparently at the mercy of her adversary and unable to obtain help. Let us, when we pray for His church or any portion of it under the power of the world, ask Him to visit her with the mighty workings of His Spirit and to prepare her for His coming. Let us pray with assured faith that prayer does help, praying always and not fainting will bring the answer. Only give God time. Then keep crying day and night. "And will not God bring about justice for his chosen ones, who cry out to him day and night? . . . I tell you, he will see that they get justice, and quickly."

O Lord my God, teach me to know your way and in faith to grasp what your beloved Son has taught us: "He will see that they get justice, and quickly." Let your tender love and the delight you have in hearing and blessing your children lead me to accept implicitly your promise that we receive what we believe, that we have the petitions we ask, and that in due time the answer will come.

Lord, help us to understand the seasons in nature and know to wait with patience for the fruit we long for. Fill us with the assurance that you will not delay one moment longer than is needed, and that faith will yield the answer.

Blessed Master, you have said that it is typical of God's elect that they cry day and night in prayer. Teach us to understand this. You know how quickly we grow faint and weary. It seems as if you are so much beyond the need or the reach of continued supplication that it is improper for us to be too importunate. Lord, teach me how real the labor of prayer is. Here on earth when I have failed in an undertaking, I can often succeed by renewed and continuing effort, by giving more time and thought to a thing. Show me how by giving myself completely to prayer and to live more in the spirit of prayer, I will obtain what I ask. Above all, blessed teacher, author and perfecter of my faith, by your grace let my whole life be one of faith in the Son of God, who loved me and gave himself for me—in whom my prayer is accepted, in whom I have the assurance of the answer, from whom the answer will surely come. Lord Jesus, in this faith I will always pray and not faint. Amen.

Chapter 17

Prayer in Harmony With the Person of God

Father, I thank you that you have heard me. I knew that you always hear me.

John 11:41–42

You are My Son, today I have begotten You. Ask of Me, and I will give You the nations for Your inheritance . . .

Psalm 2:7–8 NKJV

In the New Testament we find a distinction made between faith and knowledge. "To one there is given through the Spirit the message of *wisdom*, to another the message of *knowledge* by means of the same Spirit, to another *faith* by the same Spirit" (1 Corinthians 12:8–9). In a child or a child-like Christian there may be much faith with little knowledge. Childlike simplicity accepts the truth without difficulty and often cares little to give itself or others any reason for its faith but this: God has said it. But it is the will of God that we should love and serve Him not only with all our heart but also with all our mind; that we should grow up into an insight into the divine wisdom and beauty of all His ways and words and works. Only by growing in this way will the believer be able to fully approach and rightly adore the glory of God's grace. Only in this way can our heart intelligently comprehend the treasures of wisdom and knowledge found in redemption and be prepared to enter fully into the highest note of the song that rises before the throne: "Oh, the depth of the riches of the wisdom and knowledge of God!" (Romans 11:33).

This truth has its full application in our prayer life. While prayer and faith are so simple that the newborn convert can pray with power, the doctrine of prayer presents deep problems. Is the power of prayer a reality? How can God grant to prayer such mighty power? How can the action of prayer be harmonized with the will and the decrees of God? How can God's sovereignty and our will, God's liberty and ours, be reconciled? These and other similar questions are valid subjects for Christian meditation and inquiry. The more earnestly and reverently we approach such mysteries, the more we will fall down in adoring awe to praise Him who has in prayer given such power to men.

One of the secret difficulties with regard to prayer is one that though not expressed often hinders prayer. This difficulty is derived from the perfection of God, in His absolute independence of all that is outside of himself. Is He not the Infinite Being, who owes what He is to himself alone, who determines himself, and whose wise and holy will has determined all that is to be? How can prayer influence Him or He be moved by prayer to do what otherwise would not be done? Is not the promise of an answer to prayer simply condescension to our weakness? Is what is said of the much-availing power of prayer anything more than an accommodation to our way of thinking, since God can never be dependent on any action from without for His doings? Is not the blessing of prayer simply the influence it exercises upon *us*?

In seeking an answer to such questions, we find the key in the very being of God, in the mystery of the Holy Trinity. If God were only one person, shut up within himself, there could be no thought of nearness to Him or influence on Him. But in God there are *three* persons. In God we have Father and Son, who have in the Holy Spirit their living bond of unity and fellowship. When eternal Love begat the Son, and the Father gave the Son as the second person a place next to himself as His equal and His counselor, there was a way opened for prayer and its influence in the very inmost life of God itself.

Just as on earth, so in heaven, the whole relationship between Father and Son is that of giving and taking. And if that taking is to be as voluntary and self-determined as the giving, there must be on the part of the Son an asking and receiving. In the holy fellowship of the divine persons, this asking of the Son was one of the great operations of the thrice-blessed life of God. We see it in Psalm 2: "Today I have begotten you. Ask of me, and I will give you . . ." The Father gave the Son the place and the power to act upon Him. The asking of the Son was no mere show or shadow, but one of those life-movements in which the love of the Father and the Son met and completed each other. The Father had determined that He should not be alone in His counsels: there was a Son on whose asking and accepting their fulfillment should depend. So there was in the very being and life of God an asking of which prayer on earth was to be the reflection and the outflow. It was not without including this that Jesus said,

"I knew that you always hear me." Just as the sonship of Jesus on earth may not be separated from His sonship in heaven, even so His prayer on earth is the continuation and counterpart of His asking in heaven. The prayer of the man Christ Jesus is the link between the eternal asking of the only-begotten Son in the bosom of the Father and the prayer of humankind upon earth. Prayer has its rise and its deepest source in the very being of God. In the bosom of Deity nothing is ever done without prayer—the asking of the Son and the giving of the Father.

This may help us somewhat to understand how our prayers, coming through the Son, can have an effect upon God. The decrees of God are not decisions made by Him without reference to the Son or His petition to be sent up through Him. The Lord Jesus is the first begotten, the head and heir of all things: all things were created *through Him* and *unto Him*, and all things consist *in Him*. In the counsels of the Father, the Son, as representative of all creation, has liberty as mediator and intercessor in the petitions of all who draw near to the Father in the Son.

If we think this liberty and power of the Son to act upon the Father is at variance with the immutability of the divine decrees, let us not forget that with God there is no past to which He is irrevocably bound, as is the case with man. God does not live in time with its past and future. The distinctions of time have no reference to Him who inhabits eternity. Eternity is an ever-present *now*, in which the past is never past and the future is always present. To meet our human weakness, Scripture must speak of past decrees and a coming future. In reality, the immutability of God's counsel is always in perfect harmony with His liberty to do whatsoever He will. The prayers of the Son and His people were not taken up into the eternal decrees so that their effect should only be an apparent one. Instead, the Father-heart holds itself open and free to listen to every prayer that rises through the Son; God does indeed allow himself to be decided by prayer to do what He otherwise would not have done.

This perfect harmony and union of divine sovereignty and human liberty is to us an unfathomable mystery, because God as the Eternal One transcends all our thoughts. But be assured that in the eternal fellowship of the Father and the Son the power of prayer has its origin and certainty, and through our union with the Son our prayer is received and can have influence in the inner life of the blessed Trinity!

God's decrees are not an iron framework against which man's liberty vainly seeks to struggle. God himself is the living Love, who in His Son, as man, has entered into a tender relationship with all that is human. God through the Holy Spirit takes our humanness into the divine life of love and frees himself to give every human prayer its place in His government of the world.

It is in the revelation of such thoughts that the doctrine of the Trinity is no longer an abstract speculation, but the living manifestation of the way it is possible for man to be in fellowship with God and his prayer to become a factor in God's rule of this earth. We can, as though from a distance, catch a glimpse of the light that from eternal glory shines on words such as these: "Through him we both have access to the Father by one Spirit" (Ephesians 2:18).

This simple view of prayer is seen throughout Scripture: God hears us. It does not dwell on the reflex influence of prayer on our heart and life, although it abundantly shows the connection between prayer as an act and prayer as a state. Rather, it fixes or defines the objective or purpose of prayer: to obtain blessing, gifts, and deliverances from God. Jesus said, "Ask and it shall be given."

The following is adapted from *The Hidden Life* and *The Lord's Prayer* by A. Saphir (no publication data available).

However true and valuable the reflection may be that God, foreseeing and foreordaining all things, has also foreseen and foreordained our prayers as links in the chain of events, of cause and effect, as a real power, yet we feel convinced that this is not the light in which the mind can find peace on this great subject, nor do we think that this is the attraction to draw us to prayer. We feel rather that such a reflection *diverts* the attention from the Object from whom comes the impulse, life, and strength of prayer. The living God, contemporary, yet eternal, the living, merciful, Holy One, God manifesting himself to the soul; God saying, "Seek my face"; this is the magnet that draws us, this alone can open the heart and the voice. . . .

In Jesus Christ the Son of God, we have the full solution for the difficulty. He prayed on earth, not merely as man, but as the Son of God incarnate. His prayer on earth is only the manifestation of His prayer from all eternity, when in the divine counsel He was set up as the Christ. . . . The Son was appointed heir of all things. From all eternity the Son of God was the way, the mediator. He was, to use our imperfect language, from eternity speaking unto the Father on behalf of the world.

Everlasting God, the Three-in-One, in deep reverence I would worship before the holy mystery of your divine Being. If it should please you, most glorious God, to unveil anything of that mystery, I would bow with fear and trembling and meditate on your glory.

Father, I thank you that you bear this name not only as the

Father of your children here on earth but also as having from eternity subsisted as the Father with your only-begotten Son. I thank you that as Father you can hear our prayers because you have from eternity given a place in your counsels to the asking of your Son. I thank you that we have seen in Him on earth the blessed relationship He had with you in heaven and how from eternity in all your counsels and decrees there was room left for His prayers and their answers. And I thank you above all that through His true human nature on your throne above, and through your Holy Spirit in our human nature here below, a way has been opened by which every human cry can be received into the life and love of God and receive an answer.

Blessed Jesus, in whom as the Son the path of prayer has been opened up, and who gives us assurance of the answer, we beseech you to teach your people to pray. Each day let this be the sign of our own sonship: that like you we know that the Father always hears us. Amen.

Chapter 18

Prayer in Harmony With the Destiny of Man

And he asked them, "Whose portrait is this?
And whose inscription?"

Matthew 22:20

Then God said, "Let us make man in our image, in our likeness."

Genesis 1:26

"Whose portrait is this?" By this question Jesus foiled His enemies when they planned to trick Him, and He settled the matter of duty in regard to the tribute. The question and the principle it involves are of universal application, nowhere more truly than in man himself. The image he bears decides his destiny. Bearing God's image, he belongs to God. Prayer to God is what he was created for. Prayer is part of the wonderful likeness he bears to His divine original; of the deep mystery of the fellowship of love in which the triune God has His blessedness, prayer is the earthly image and likeness.

The more we meditate on what prayer is, and its wonderful power with God, the more we feel constrained to ask, "Who—and what—is man that such a place in God's counsels should have been allotted to him?" (cf. Psalm

8:4–8). Sin has so degraded him that from what he is now we can form no conception of what he was meant to be. We must turn back to God's own record of man's creation to discover what God's purpose was and what capacities man was endowed with for the fulfillment of that purpose.

Man's destiny appears clearly from God's language at creation. It was to *fill*, to *subdue*, and to *have dominion* over the earth and all that is in it. All three expressions show us that man was meant to rule here on earth as God's representative. As God's viceroy, he was to fill God's place. Subject to God, he was to keep all else in subjection to Him. It was the will of God that all that was to be done on earth should be done through man. The history of the earth was to be entirely in his hands.

In accordance with such a destiny was the position he was to occupy and the power that was at his disposal. When an earthly sovereign sends a representative to a distant province, it is understood that he advises as to the policy to be adopted and that advice is acted on. He is at liberty to apply for troops and the other means needed for carrying out the policy or maintaining the dignity of the empire. If his policy is not approved, he is recalled, to make way for someone who better understands his sovereign's desires. As long as he is trusted, his advice is carried out. As God's representative, man was to have ruled. On his advice and at his request, heaven was to have bestowed its blessing on earth. His prayer was to have been the wonderful, though simple and most natural channel, in which the close relationship between the King in heaven and man, His faithful servant as lord of this world, was to have been maintained. The destinies of the world were given into the power of the wishes, the will, and the prayer of man.

Of course, with the entrance of sin into the picture, this plan underwent a catastrophic change: man's fall brought all creation under the curse. With redemption, the beginning of a glorious restoration was seen. No sooner had God begun in Abraham to form for himself a people from whom kings—even the great King—should come forth than we see what power the prayer of God's faithful servant has to decide the destinies of those who come into contact with him. In Abraham we see how prayer is not only, or even chiefly, the means of obtaining blessing for ourselves. Rather, it is the exercise of his royal prerogative to influence the destinies of men and the will of God that rules them. Not once do we find Abraham praying for himself. His prayer for Sodom and Lot, for Abimelech, and for Ishmael, prove what power a man who is God's friend has to create the history of those around him.

This had been man's destiny from the start. Scripture not only tells us this but also teaches us how it was that God could entrust man with such a high calling. It was because He had created him in His own image and likeness. The external rule was not committed to him without the inner fitness. Bearing God's image in having dominion, in being lord of all, had its root in the inner likeness, in his nature. An inner agreement and harmony existed between God and man, an incipient godlikeness, which fitted man to be the mediator between God and His world. Since he was to be prophet, priest, and king, he was to interpret God's will, to represent nature's needs, to receive and dispense God's bounty. In bearing God's image, he could bear God's rule. Indeed, he was so like God, so capable of entering into God's purposes and carrying out His plans, that God could trust him with the wonderful privilege of asking and obtaining what the world might need.

Although sin has for a time frustrated God's plans, prayer still remains what it would have been if man had never fallen—the proof of man's godlikeness, his link with the infinite unseen One, the power that is allowed to hold the hand that holds the destinies of the universe. Prayer is not merely the cry of the supplicant for mercy; it is the highest expression of His will by man, who knows himself to be of divine origin, created for and capable of being, in king-like liberty, the executor of the counsels of the Eternal.

What sin destroyed, grace has restored. What the first Adam lost, the second has won back. In Christ man regains his original position, and the church, abiding in Christ, inherits the promise "Ask whatever you wish, and it will be given you" (John 15:7).

By no means does such a promise refer primarily to the grace or blessing we need for ourselves. It refers to our position as fruit-bearing branches of the heavenly Vine, who, like Him, live only for the work and glory of the Father. It is for those who abide in Him, who have forsaken self to abide in Him with His life of obedience and self-sacrifice, those who have lost their life and found it in Him, and are now entirely given up to the interests of the Father and His kingdom. These are they who understand how their new creation has brought them back to their original destiny, has restored God's image and likeness, and with it the power to have dominion. Such have indeed the power, each in their own circle, to obtain and dispense the powers of heaven here on earth. With holy boldness they may make known what they will. They live as priests in God's presence. As kings the powers of the world to come begin to be at their disposal.* They enter upon the fulfillment of the promise: "Ask whatever you wish, and it will be given you" (John 15:7).

Church of the living God, your calling is higher and holier than you know. Through your members, as kings and priests unto God, would God rule the world; their prayers bestow and withhold the blessings of heaven. His elect are not simply content to be saved. Instead, they yield themselves wholly, that through them, just as through the Son, the Father may fulfill all His glorious counsel. In these His elect, who cry day and night unto Him, God would prove how wonderful man's original destiny was.

As the image-bearer of God on earth, the earth was indeed given into man's hands. When he fell, all fell with him; the whole creation groans and travails in pain together. But now he is redeemed, and the restoration of the original dignity has begun. It is God's purpose that the fulfillment of His eternal purpose and the coming of His kingdom should depend on those of His people who, abiding in Christ, are ready to take up their position in Him their head, the great Priest-King, and in their prayers are bold enough to say what they will that their God should do. As image-bearer and representative of God on earth, redeemed man by his prayers

---

*God is seeking priests among the sons of men. A human priesthood is one of the essential parts of His eternal plan. To rule creation by man is His design; to carry on the worship of creation by man is no less part of His design.

Priesthood is the appointed link between heaven and earth, the channel of communication between the sinner and God. Such a priesthood, insofar as expiation is concerned, is in the hands of the Son of God alone; insofar as it is to be the medium of communication between Creator and creature, it is also in the hands of redeemed men—of the church of God.

God is seeking kings not from the ranks of angels; fallen man must furnish Him with the rulers of His universe. Human hands must wield the scepter; human heads must wear the crown. (Adapted from Dr. H. Bonar, *The Rent Veil*. No publication data available).

determines the history of this earth. Man was created and has been redeemed to pray, and by his prayer to have dominion.

Lord, what is man that you are mindful of him? And the son of man, that you visit him? You have made him a little lower than the angels, and have crowned him with glory and honor. You made him to have dominion over the work of your hands. You have put all things under his feet. O Lord, our Lord, how excellent is your name in all the earth!

Lord God, how low sin has made men sink. How it has darkened his mind that he does not even know his divine destiny: to be your servant and representative. How sad that even your people, when their eyes are opened, are so slow to accept their calling and seek to have power with God in order to have power with men and to bless them.

Lord Jesus, in you the Father has crowned man with glory and honor and opened the way for us to be what He would have us to be. O Lord, have mercy on your people, and visit your heritage! Work mightily in your church and teach your believing disciples to go forth in their royal priesthood and in the power of prayer, to which you have given such wonderful promises. Teach them to serve your kingdom, to have rule over the nations, and make the name of God glorious in the earth. Amen.

Chapter 19

Power for Prayer and Work

I tell you the truth, anyone who has faith in me will do what I have been doing. He will do even greater things than these, because I am going to the Father. And I will do whatever you ask in my name.

John 14:12–13

The Savior opened His public ministry with His disciples with the Sermon on the Mount. Now He closes it by the parting address preserved for us by John. In both He speaks more than once of prayer—but with a difference. The Sermon on the Mount is to disciples who have just entered His school, who scarcely know that God is their Father, and whose prayer's chief reference is to their personal needs. In His closing address, He speaks to disciples whose training time has now come to an end, and who are ready as His messengers to take His place and do His work. In the former, the chief lesson is to be childlike, to pray in faith, and to trust the Father to give you good gifts. Now He points to something higher. Now they are His friends to whom He has made known all He has heard from His Father. They are His messengers who have entered into His plans and into whose hands the care of His work and kingdom on earth is to be entrusted. They are to go out and do His work, and in the power of His approaching exaltation even greater works. Prayer is to be the channel through which that power is received for their work. With Christ's ascension to the Father, a new epoch begins, both for their work and for their life of prayer.

How clearly this connection comes out in our text. As Christ's body here on earth, as those who are one with Him in heaven, the disciples are now to do greater works than He had done. Their success and their victories are to be greater than His. He mentions two reasons for this. First, because He was to go to the Father to receive all power. Second, because they might now ask and expect anything in His name. "Because I am going to the Father. *And* I will do whatever you ask in my name." His going to the Father would in this way bring a double blessing. They would ask and receive all in His name, and as a consequence be able to do the greater works. The first mention of prayer in our Savior's parting words teaches us two important lessons. He that would do the works of Jesus *must pray*. He that would pray in His name *must work*.

He who would work *must pray*. In prayer, power for work is obtained. As long as Jesus was here on earth, He did the greatest works. The same demons that the disciples could not cast out fled at His word. When Jesus went to the Father, He was no longer here in body to do the work. The disciples became His body. All His work from the throne must and could be done through them.

One might have thought with His leaving the scene and

only working through commissioners, the work might suffer—become less and be weaker. He assures us of the contrary: "I tell you *the truth*, anyone who has faith in me will do what I have been doing. He will do even greater things than these" (John 14:12). His approaching death was to break down and bring to an end the power of sin. With the Resurrection, the power of eternal life was to take possession of the human body and to obtain supremacy over human life. With His ascension, He was to receive the power to communicate the Holy Spirit to His own. The union between himself on the throne and those on earth was to be so intense and so divinely perfect that He meant it literally when He said: "He will do even greater things than these, because I am going to the Father" (John 14:12). And the results proved how true it was.

During the three years of His personal labor on earth, Jesus gathered few more than five hundred disciples, and most of them so frail that they were only a small credit to His cause. Men like Peter and Paul were allowed to do greater things than He did. From the throne Jesus could do through them what on earth He alone could not do.

But there is one condition: "Anyone who has *faith* in me will do . . . even greater things than these, because I am going to the Father. And I will do whatever you ask in my name" (John 14:12–13). His going to the Father would give Him new power to hear prayer. Two things were needed for doing the greater works: His going to the Father to receive all power, and our prayer of faith in His name to receive all power from Him. As He asks the Father, He receives and bestows on us the power of the new dispensation for the greater works. As we believe, and ask in His name, the power takes possession of us to do the greater works.

How much striving there is in the work of God where there is little or nothing to be seen of the power to do anything like Christ's works, not to mention greater works. There can be only one reason: believing prayer in His name is lacking.

How wonderful if every laborer and leader in the churches, schools, and mission outreaches would learn this lesson: Prayer in Jesus' name is the way to share in the power Jesus has received from the Father for His people. In this power the one who believes can do the greater works. To every complaint of weakness or inadequacy, difficulty or lack of success, Jesus has one answer: "Anyone who has faith in me will do . . . even greater things, because I am going to the Father. And I will do whatever you ask in my name" (John 14:12–13). We must understand that the most important thing for anyone who desires to do the work of Jesus is to believe, becoming linked to Him, and then to pray the prayer of faith in His name. Without this act of faith our work is merely human, carnal. It may help to restrain sin or to prepare the way for blessing, but power is lacking. Powerful, effective work first needs powerful, effective prayer.

In contrast to prayer before work, one must work after the prayer is done. Prayer enables us to work effectively. Both are necessary to the success of the kingdom.

In these parting words of our Lord, He no less than six times (John 14:13–14; 15:7, 16; 16:23–24) repeats the unlimited prayer-promises that have often stirred anxious doubts as to their true meaning: *I will do whatever you ask, You may ask me for anything, Ask whatever you wish, The Father will give you whatever you ask, Ask and you will receive, and your joy will be complete.* How many believers have read these statements with joy and hope, and in deep earnestness of soul have sought to plead them—only to come away disappointed? The simple reason is that they have separated the promise from its context. The Lord gave the wonderful promise of the free use of His name before the Father in connection with *doing His works*. It is the disciple who gives himself wholly to live for Jesus' work and kingdom, for His will and honor, to whom the power will come to appropriate the promise. He who tries to grasp the promise when he wants something solely for himself will be disappointed, because he is trying to make Jesus the servant of his own comfort. But the one who seeks to pray the effective prayer of faith because he needs it for the work of the Master, will learn its power—because he has made himself the servant of his Lord's interests. Not only does prayer strengthen us for the work but work strengthens us for prayer.

This is in perfect harmony with a truth in both the natural and the spiritual world: "Whoever has will be given more" (Mark 4:25); or, "Whoever can be trusted with very little can also be trusted with much" (Luke 16:10). With the small measure of grace already received, we should give ourselves to the Master for His work. Work will then be to us a school of prayer. When Moses had full charge of a rebellious people, he felt the need—but also the courage—to speak boldly to God and to ask great things of Him (Exodus 33:12, 15, 18). As you give yourself entirely to God for His work, you will feel that nothing less than these great promises are what you need, and that nothing less is what you may confidently expect.

You are called and appointed to do the works of Jesus, and even greater works, because He has gone to the Father to receive the power to do them in and through you. "And *I will do whatever* you ask in my name" (John 14:13). Give yourself, and live, to do the works of Christ, and you will learn to pray so that you obtain wonderful answers to prayer. Give yourself, and live, to pray and you will do the works He did—and greater works. With disciples full of faith in Him and bold in prayer to ask great things, Christ can conquer the world.

Lord, again today I have heard words from you that are beyond my comprehension. And yet I can do nothing except in simple, childlike faith take and keep them as your gifts to me. You have said that because of your going to the Father, he that believes in you will do the works that you have done, and greater works. Lord, I worship you as the glorified One, and look for the fulfillment of your promise. May my whole life be one of continued believing in you. Purify and sanctify my heart and make it sensitive to you and your love, so that believing in you may be its very life.

You have said that because of your going to the Father you will do whatsoever we ask in your name. From your throne you would share the power given you with your people and work through them as the members of your body in response to their believing prayers. Power in prayer with you and power in work with others is what you have promised your people.

Blessed Lord, forgive us for not always believing you and your promise, and for so seldom proving your faithfulness in fulfilling it.

Teach me to pray so that I may prove that your name is all-powerful with God, with men, and with demons. Teach me to so pray that you can glorify yourself and do your great works through me. Amen.

Chapter 20

The Chief End of Prayer

I am going to the Father. And I will do whatever you ask in my name, so that the Son may bring glory to the Father.

John 14:12–13

That the Son may bring glory to the Father. For this reason Jesus on His throne in glory will do all we ask in His name. Every answer to prayer He gives will have this as its object: when there is no prospect of the Father being glorified, He will not answer. As with Jesus, the essential element in our petitions must be the glory of the Father—the aim, the end, the very soul and life of our prayer.

When Jesus was on earth, He said, "For I have come down from heaven not to do my will but to do the will of him who sent me" (John 6:38). In these words we have the keynote of His life. In the first words of the high-priestly prayer He expresses it as well: "Father . . . glorify your Son, that your Son may glorify you" (John 17:1). "I have brought you glory on earth . . . glorify me in your presence" (John 17:4–5). The ground on which He asks to be taken into glory is twofold: He has glorified Him on earth; He will glorify Him in heaven. What He asks is only to enable Him to glorify the Father more. As we agree with Jesus on this point, and please Him by making the Father's glory our chief object too, our prayer cannot fail to be answered.

Jesus said that nothing glorifies the Father more than His doing what we ask. He will not, therefore, let any opportunity slip by for answering these prayers. Let us make His aim ours. Let the glory of the Father be the link between our asking and His doing. Prayer like that must prevail.

This word of Jesus comes indeed as a sharp two-edged sword, piercing even to the dividing of soul and spirit, and is quick to discern the thoughts and intents of the heart. Jesus in His prayers on earth, in His intercession in heaven, and in His promise of an answer to our prayers, makes this His first object—the glory of His Father. Is it so with us? Or are self-interest and self-will the strongest motives that urge us to pray? Or, if not, do we have to confess that the distinct, conscious longing for the glory of the Father is not what animates our prayers?

Not that the believer does not at times want to pray with that motive, but he grieves that he seldom does. He knows the reason for his failure: the gulf between the spirit of daily life and the spirit of prayer was too great. We begin to see that the desire for the glory of the Father is not something that we can stir up and present to our Lord only when we prepare ourselves to pray. Only when the whole life, in all its parts, is surrendered to God's glory can we really pray to His glory. "*Do it all* for the glory of God" (1 Corinthians 10:31), and "*Ask all* to the glory of God"—these twin commands are inseparable. Obedience to the former is the secret of grace for the latter. A life yielded to the glory of God is the condition for the prayers that Jesus can answer.

This demand in connection with prevailing prayer—that

it should be to the glory of God—is no more than right and natural. There is none glorious but the Lord; there is no glory except His and what He gives to His creatures. Creation exists to show forth His glory. All that is not for His glory is sin and darkness and death. Only in glorifying God can creatures find glory. What the Son of Man did—give His whole life to glorify the Father—is the simple duty of everyone who is redeemed. He will also share Christ's reward. Because Christ gave himself so entirely to the glory of the Father, the Father crowned him with glory and honor, giving the kingdom into His hands with power to ask what He will, and as Intercessor to answer our prayers. And just as we become one with Christ in this, and as our prayer is part of a life utterly surrendered to God's glory, so will the Savior be able to glorify the Father to us by the fulfillment of the promise "I will do whatever you ask" (John 14:13).

A life with God's glory as our only aim cannot be attained by any effort of our own. Only in Christ Jesus is such a life seen, but through Him it is also possible for us. Yes, blessed be God! His life is our life.

The discovery of self as usurping the place of God and the confession and denial of self-seeking and self-trusting is essential—but we cannot accomplish it in our own strength. Only Jesus can cast out the self-glorifying life and give us His own God-glorifying life and Spirit. As His presence comes in to dwell and reign in our hearts, Jesus who longs to glorify the Father by hearing our prayers will teach us to live and pray to the glory of God.

What motivation will urge our slothful hearts to yield themselves to our Lord to work this in us? Surely nothing more is needed than a vision of how gloriously worthy the Father is. Let our faith learn to bow before Him in adoring worship and ascribe to Him alone the kingdom, the power, and the glory. May we yield ourselves to dwell in His light as the ever-blessed, ever-loving One. Surely we will be moved to say, "To him be glory both now and forever" (2 Peter 3:18). Then we will look to our Lord Jesus with a new desire for a life that refuses to seek anything other than the glory of God.

When there is only prayer that cannot be answered, the Father is not glorified. It is our duty to live and pray so that our prayer can be answered and so glorify God. For the sake of God's glory, let us learn how to pray.

How humbling that so often our joy or pleasure in prayer for someone or something is far stronger than our yearning for God's glory. No wonder there are so many unanswered prayers. Here is the secret: God cannot be glorified when His glory is not our object. He who would pray the prayer of faith must live so that the Father is glorified in him in all things. This must be his aim. Without this, there can be no prayer of faith.

"How can you believe," Jesus asked, "if you accept praise from one another, yet make no effort to obtain the praise that comes from the only God?" (John 5:44). Seeking our own glory with men makes faith impossible. The deep self-sacrifice that gives up its own glory and seeks the glory of God alone, and that awakens in the soul spiritual sensitivity to the divine—that is faith. Surrender to God to seek His glory and the expectation that He will display His glory in hearing us are one. He that seeks God's glory will see it in the answer to his prayer.

But how shall we attain to it? Let us begin with confession. Has the glory of God been an all-absorbing passion? Have our lives and our prayers been filled with it? Have we lived in the likeness of the Son and in agreement with Him—for God and His glory alone?

Let us wait on God in prayer until the Holy Spirit reveals it to us and we see how we have sinned in this regard. True knowledge and confession of sin is the sure path to deliverance.

Looking to Jesus, we can see by what death we can glorify God. In death He glorified Him. Through death He was glorified with Him. By dying, being dead to self and living to God, we can glorify Him. This death to self, this life to the glory of God, is what Jesus gives and lives in each one who can trust Him for it. Let nothing less than these—the desire and decision to live only for the glory of the Father as Christ did; the acceptance of Him with His life and strength working it in us; the joyful assurance that we can live to the glory of God because Christ lives in us—let this be the spirit of our daily life. Jesus stands to support our living in this way. The Holy Spirit is given and waiting to make it our experience, if we will only trust and let Him. Let us not hold back through unbelief, but confidently take as our watchword: *All* to the glory of God! The Father accepts the will, and the sacrifice is pleasing to Him. Then the Holy Spirit will seal us within with the consciousness that we are living for God and His glory.

What quiet peace and power there will be in our prayers when we know ourselves, through His grace, to be in perfect harmony with Him who promises to do what we ask: "That the Son may bring glory to the Father" (John 14:13). With our whole being consciously yielded to the inspiration of the Word and Spirit, our desires will be no longer ours but His, with their chief end the glory of God. With increasing liberty we shall be able to pray: "Father, you know that we ask it only for your glory."

The condition for answers to prayer, instead of being like a mountain we cannot climb, will give us the greater confidence that we will be heard, because we have seen that prayer has no higher blessedness than that it glorifies the Father. And the precious privilege of prayer will become doubly precious because it brings us into perfect unison with the Son in the wonderful partnership He proposes: "*You ask*, and *I do*, that the Son may bring glory to the Father."

Blessed Lord Jesus, I come again to you. Every lesson you teach convinces me more deeply how little I know how to pray in the right way. But every lesson also inspires me with hope that you are going to teach me and that you are teaching me not only what prayer should be but also how to pray as I ought. Lord, I look with courage to you—the great Intercessor, who prays and hears prayer—only for the Father to be glorified. Teach me also to live and to pray to the glory of God.

To this end I yield myself to you again. I would be nothing. I have given self to death, as already crucified with you. Through the Spirit, self's workings have come to nothing. Your life and your love of the Father are taking possession of me. A new longing begins to fill my soul that every day, every hour, in every prayer, the glory of the Father may be everything to me. Lord, I am in your school to learn this. Teach me.

God of glory, the Father of glory, my God and my Father, accept the desire of a child who has seen that your glory alone is worth living for. Lord, show me your glory. Let it overshadow me. Let it fill the temple of my heart. Let me dwell in it as revealed in Christ. Fulfill in me your own good pleasure, that your child should find glory in seeking the glory of the Father. Amen.

Chapter 21

The All-Inclusive Condition

If you abide in me, and my words abide in you, ask whatever you wish, and it shall be done for you.

John 15:7 NASB

In all God's dealings with us, the promise and its conditions are inseparable. If we fulfill the conditions, He fulfills the promise. What He is to be to us depends upon what we are willing to be to Him. "Come near to God and he will come near to you" (James 4:8). And so in prayer the unlimited promise "Ask whatever you wish" has one simple and natural condition: "if you abide in me." The Father always hears His Son. God is *in Christ*, and can be reached only because He is in Him. To be *in Him* is the way to have our prayers heard. Fully and wholly *abiding in Him*, we have the right to ask whatsoever we will and the promise that it will be done for us.

When we compare this promise with the experience of most believers, we are startled by an awesome discrepancy. Who could count the prayers that rise to God and have no answer? Why is this? Either we do not fulfill the condition or God does not fulfill the promise.

Believers are not willing to admit either, and therefore have devised a way of escape from the dilemma. They add to the promise the qualifying clause our Savior did not put there: if it is God's will. That way, they maintain both God's integrity and their own. How sad that they do not accept and hold the Word as it stands, trusting Christ to vindicate His truth. Then God's Spirit would lead them to see the divine propriety of such a promise to those who truly abide in Christ in the sense in which He means it, and to confess that the failure in fulfilling the condition is the one sufficient explanation of unanswered prayer. The Holy Spirit would then make our weakness in prayer one of the motives to urge us on to discover the secret and obtain the blessing of full abiding in Christ.

"If you abide in me." As a Christian grows in grace and in the knowledge of the Lord Jesus, he is often surprised to find how the words of God grow in new and deeper meaning for him. He can look back to the day when some word of God was opened up to him and the blessing he found in it. After a time some deeper experience gave it a new meaning, and it was as if he had never seen it before. Again, as he advances in the Christian life, the same word may come to him as a great mystery until the Holy Spirit leads him still deeper into its divine fullness. One of these ever-growing, never-exhausted words that opens up to us step by step the fullness of the divine life is the Master's "Abide in me." As the union of the branch with the vine is one of unceasing growth and increase, so our abiding in Christ is a life process in which the divine life takes ever fuller and more complete possession of us. The young or the weak believer may be

abiding in Christ to the measure of his light; he who reaches beyond to the full abiding in the sense in which the Master understood the words, is the one who inherits all the promises connected with it.

In the growing life of abiding in Christ, the first stage is that of faith. The believer sees that in spite of all his frailty, the command is really meant for him. Then his aim is simply to believe that just as he knows he is in Christ, so in spite of failure, abiding in Christ is his immediate duty and within his reach. He is especially occupied with the love, power, and faithfulness of the Savior. He feels his immediate need is to simply believe.

Before long he sees something more is needed. Obedience and faith must go together. It is not as if obedience is added to the faith he has, but faith must be seen in his obedience. Faith is active in obedience in the home; then obedience is faith stepping out to do His will. He sees how he has been more occupied with the privilege and the blessings of this abiding than with its duties and its fruit. There has been evidence of self and of self-will that has gone unnoticed or tolerated. The peace that as a young or a weak disciple he could enjoy in believing evades him. It is in practical obedience that the abiding must be maintained: "If you obey my commands, you will remain in my love" (John 15:10). Before his great aim was to let his heart rest in Christ and His promises through the *mind* and the truth it was able to grasp. Now in this stage his chief effort is to unite his *will* with the will of his Lord and allow the heart and the life to be brought entirely under His rule.

But it seems there is something missing. The will and the heart are on Christ's side. He obeys and he loves his Lord. But why is it that the fleshly nature still has so much power?

Or why are the spontaneous actions and emotions of the inmost being not what they should be? The will does not approve or allow it, but here is a region beyond control of the will. Why also—even when there is not so much of positive commission to condemn—is there so much omission, so much deficiency of that beauty of holiness? Where is that zeal of love, that conformity to Jesus and His death in which the life of self is lost, and which is surely implied in abiding as the Master described it? There must surely be something in our abiding in Christ and Christ in us that a young Christian has not yet experienced.

Faith and obedience are only the pathway to blessing. Before giving us the parable of the vine and the branches, Jesus very distinctly told us what the full blessing is toward which faith and obedience should lead. Three times He said, "If you love me, you will obey what I command" (John 14:15), and spoke of the threefold blessing with which He would crown such obedient love. The Holy Spirit would come from the Father; the Son would manifest himself; the Father and the Son would come and make their abode.

As our faith grows into obedience, our whole being clings to Christ in love. Our inner life opens up and the capacity is formed within us to receive the life and spirit of the glorified Jesus. The word is fulfilled in us: "On that day you will realize that I am in my Father, and you are in me, and I am in you" (John 14:20).

We see that just as Christ is in God and God in Christ, not only one in will and in love but also in identity of nature and life because they exist in each other, so we are in Christ and Christ in us, a union not only of will and love but also of life and nature.

After Jesus spoke of our knowing through the Holy Spirit

that He is in the Father and we are in Him and He in us, He said, "Abide in Me, and I in you" (John 15:4 NKJV). In other words, accept, consent, to receive that divine life of union with Him. As you abide in Him, He also will abide in you even as He abides in the Father.

This is occupying the position in which Christ can come and abide; abiding in Him so that the soul draws away from self and finds that He has taken its place and become our life. It is becoming like little children who have no cares and find their happiness in trusting and obeying the love that has done everything for them.

To those who abide like this, the promise comes as their rightful heritage: Ask whatever you wish. It cannot be otherwise. Christ has full possession of them. Christ dwells in their love, their will, their life. Not only has their will been given up but Christ has entered it. There He dwells and breathes into it His Spirit. He whom the Father always hears, prays through them. What they ask will be done for them.

Fellow believer, let us confess that it is because we do not abide in Christ that the church is so impotent in the face of unfaithfulness, worldliness, and unbelief.

But let us not be discouraged. The abiding of the branch in the Vine is a life of never-ending growth. Abiding as the Master meant for us to abide is within our reach, for He lives to give it to us. Only let us be ready to count all things loss and say, "Not that I have already obtained all this . . . but I press on to take hold of that for which Christ Jesus took hold of me" (Philippians 3:12). Let us not be so much occupied with the abiding as with *Him* to whom the abiding links us. Let it be *Him*, the whole Christ, in His obedience and humiliation, in His exaltation and power, in whom our soul moves and acts. He himself will fulfill His promise in us.

As we abide and continue to grow in our abiding, let us exercise our right—the choice to enter into all of God's will. Obeying what that will commands, let us also claim what it promises. Let us yield to the teaching of the Holy Spirit, who shows each of us, according to His measure, what we may claim in prayer as God's will for us. Let us rest content with nothing less than the personal experience of what Jesus gave when He said, "If you abide in me, and my words abide in you, ask whatever you wish, and it shall be done for you" (John 15:7 NASB).

On a thoughtful comparison of what we mostly find in books or sermons on prayer and the teaching of the Master, we will find one great difference: the importance assigned to the answer to prayer is by no means the same. In the former we find a great deal on the blessing of prayer as a spiritual exercise even if there is no answer and on the reasons why we should be content without one. It says God's fellowship ought to be more to us than the gift we ask; God's wisdom only knows what is best; God may bestow something better than what He withholds. Though this teaching looks very high and spiritual, it is remarkable that we find nothing of it from our Lord. The more carefully we gather together all He spoke on prayer, the clearer it becomes that He wanted us to think of prayer simply as the means to an end, and that the answer was to be the proof that we and our prayer are acceptable to the Father in heaven. It is not that Christ would have us count the gifts of higher value than the fellowship and favor of the Father, but the Father intends the answer to be the token of his favor and of the reality of our fellowship with Him. "Today your servant knows that he has found favor in your eyes, my lord the king, because the king has granted his servant's request" (2 Samuel 14:22).

A life marked by daily answers to prayer is the proof of spiritual maturity: that we have indeed attained to the true abiding in Christ; that our will is truly at one with God's will; that our faith has grown strong to see and take what God has prepared for us; that the name of Christ and His nature have taken full possession of us; and that we have been found fit to take a place among those whom God admits to His counsels and according to whose prayer He rules the world. These are they in whom something of man's original dignity has been restored, in whom, as they abide in Christ, His power as the all-prevailing Intercessor can manifest itself, in whom the glory of His name is shown forth. Prayer is very blessed; *the answer is even more blessed*, as the response from the Father that our prayer, our faith, our will are indeed as He would want them to be.

I say these things to encourage you to gather all Christ's teaching about prayer and to believe the truth that when prayer is what it should be, when we are what we should be, the answer should be expected. It will bring us out from those refuges where we have comforted ourselves with unanswered prayer. It will show us the place of power to which Christ has appointed His church, and which it so little occupies. It will reveal the serious weakness of our spiritual life as the cause of our not praying boldly in Christ's name. It will urge us to rise to a life of union with Christ and fullness of the Spirit as the secret of effective prayer. It will lead us on to realize our destiny: "*In that day*: I tell you the truth, my Father will give you whatever you ask in my name. . . . Ask and you will receive, and your joy will be complete" (John 16:23). Prayer that is spiritually *in union with Jesus* is always answered.

Beloved Lord, teach me to take this promise afresh in all its simplicity and know that the only measure of your holy giving is our willingness to receive. Let each word of this promise be made vital and powerful in my soul.

You say, Abide in me! I do abide in you. Help me to grow up into all your fullness. It is not the effort of faith, seeking to cling to you, or even the rest of faith, trusting you to keep me; it is not the obedience of the will or keeping the commandments that can satisfy me. Only you living in me will satisfy me. It is you, my Lord, no longer before me and above me, but one with me, abiding in me; it is this I need, it is this I seek. It is this I trust you for.

You say, Ask whatsoever you will! Lord, I know that the life of full, deep abiding in you will renew and sanctify and strengthen my will that I will have the liberty to ask great things. Lord, let my will, renewed by your life, be bold in its petitions.

You say, It will be done. You who are the Amen, the Faithful and True Witness, give me the joyful confidence that you will make this word more wonderfully true to me than ever, because it has not entered into the heart of man to conceive what God has prepared for them that love Him. Amen.

Chapter 22

The Word and Prayer

If you abide in Me, and My words abide in you, ask whatever you wish, and it shall be done for you.

John 15:7 NASB

The vital connection between the Word and prayer is one of the simplest and earliest lessons of the Christian life. As one new convert put it: "When I pray, I speak to my Father; when I read, my Father speaks to me. Before prayer, it is God's Word that prepares me for it by revealing what the Father has told me to ask. In prayer, it is God's Word that strengthens me by giving my faith its grounds for asking. And after prayer, it is God's Word that brings me the answer, for through it the Spirit shows me I have heard the Father's voice."

Prayer is not a monologue but a dialogue; God's voice in response to mine is its most essential part. Listening to God's voice is the secret of the assurance that He will listen to mine. "Give ear and hear" (Daniel 9:18); "Give ear to my prayer" (Psalm 17:1); "Listen to my cry" (Psalm 5:2); are words that God speaks to man as well as words man speaks to God. His listening will depend on ours. To the degree that

His words find entrance into my heart will my words find effect with Him. What God's words are to me is the test of what He is to me, and also of the uprightness of my desire after Him in prayer.

Jesus points to this connection between His Word and our prayer when He says, "If you abide in Me, *and My words abide in you,* ask whatever you wish, and it shall be done for you." The deep importance of this truth becomes clear as we notice the other expression from which this one is taken. More than once Jesus said, "Abide in Me, and *I in you*" (John 15:4 NASB). His abiding in us was the complement and the crown of our abiding in Him. But here, instead of "Abide in Me, and *I in you*," He says, "You abide in Me, *and My words abide in you.*" His words abiding are the equivalent of His abiding.

What a picture is opened up to us here of the place the words of God in Christ are to have in our spiritual life, especially in prayer. By his words a man *reveals himself.* By his promises *he gives himself away*; he binds himself to the one who receives his promises. In his commands he sets forth his will and seeks *to make himself master* of him whose obedience he claims, to guide and use him as if he were part of himself. It is through our words that spirit holds fellowship with spirit and that the spirit of one man passes over to another. It is through the words of a man, heard and accepted, held fast and obeyed, that he can impart himself to another. On a human level, all this is done in a very relative and limited sense.

But when God, the infinite Being, in whom is life and power, spirit and truth—in the very deepest meaning of the words—speaks himself into His words, He really gives himself, His love and His life, His will and His power, to those who receive the words in a comprehensive way. In every promise He includes *himself* that we may lay hold of it with confidence; in every command He puts *himself* that we might share with Him His will, His holiness, and His perfection. In God's Word God gives us himself. His Word is nothing less than the eternal Son, Jesus Christ. And so all Christ's words are God's words, full of divine quickening life and power. "The words I have spoken to you are spirit and they are life" (John 6:63).

Those who study and observe hearing impairment tell us how much the power of speaking depends on hearing, and how the loss of hearing in children is followed by loss of speaking. This is true in a wider sense: as we hear, so we speak. This is true in the highest sense of our communion with God. To pray—give utterance to certain wishes and appeal to certain promises—is an easy thing, and can be learned by anyone through human wisdom. But to pray in the Spirit and speak words that reach and touch God, that affect and influence the powers of the unseen world—such praying and speaking depend entirely upon our hearing God's voice. To the degree that we listen to the voice and language God speaks, and in God's words receive His thoughts, His mind, His life, into our heart, we will learn to speak in the voice and the language that God hears. It is the ear of the learner, awakened morning by morning, that prepares for the tongue of the learned to speak to God as well as to men (Isaiah 50:4).

Hearing the voice of God is something more than the thoughtful study of the Word of God. There may be study and knowledge of the Word in which there is very little real fellowship with the living God. But there is also a reading of the Word in the very presence of the Father and under the leading of the Spirit, in which the Word becomes to us a living power from God himself. It can be to us the very voice of the Father, a kind of personal fellowship with Him. It is the living voice of God entering the heart that brings blessing and strength, awakening the response of a living faith that reaches back to God.

It is on hearing this voice that the power both to obey and to believe depends. The chief thing is not to know *what* God has said we must do but that *God* has said it. It is not the law or the book, not the knowledge of what is right that works obedience, but the personal influence of God and a living fellowship with Him. Even so, it is not the knowledge of *what* God has promised, but the *presence* of God that awakens faith and trust in prayer. It is only in the full presence of God that disobedience and unbelief become impossible.

"If you abide in Me, and My words abide in you, ask whatever you wish, and it shall be done for you." Can you see what this means? The Savior gives himself. We must have His words *in us*, accepted into our will and life, and reproduced in our disposition and conduct. We must have them *abiding* in us—our whole life one continuous exposition of the words that are within and filling us; the words revealing Christ within, and our life revealing Him without. As the words of Christ enter our heart, become our life and influence it, our words will enter His heart and influence Him. My prayer will depend on my life. What God's words are to me and in me, my words will be to God and in God. It is almost as simple as *If I do what God says, God will do what I say.*

How well the Old Testament saints understood this connection between God's words and ours, and how truly prayer for them was the loving response to what they had heard God speak! If the word were a promise, they counted on God to *do as He had spoken.* "Do as you promised" (2 Samuel 7:25); "For you, O Sovereign Lord, have spoken" (2 Samuel 7:29); "As you have promised" (Luke 2:29); "According to your word" (Psalm 119:169). By such expressions they showed that what God promised was the root and the life of what they repeated in prayer. If the word was a command, they simply *did as the Lord had spoken:* "So Abram departed as the Lord had spoken" (Genesis 12:4 NKJV). Their life was fellowship with God in an interchange of words and thoughts. What God spoke, they heard and did. What they spoke, God heard and did. In each word He speaks to us, the whole Christ gives himself to fulfill it for us. For each word He asks no less than that we give our whole person to keep that word and to receive its fulfillment.

"If . . . my words abide in you" is a simple and clear condition. In His words His will is revealed. As the words abide in me, His will rules in me. My will becomes the empty vessel that His will fills, the willing instrument that His will wields. He fills my inner being. In the exercise of obedience and faith my will becomes stronger and is brought into deeper inner harmony with Him. He can fully trust it to will nothing but what He wills. He is not afraid to give the promise "If . . . my words abide in you, ask whatever you wish, and it shall be done for you." To all who believe and act upon this promise, He will make it true.

Followers of Christ, is it not more and more clear to us that while we have been excusing our unanswered prayers and our impotence in prayer with an imagined submission to God's wisdom and will, the real reason is that our own weak spiritual life is the cause of our weak prayers?

Nothing but the word coming to us from God's mouth can make us strong. By that we must live. The word of Christ—loved, lived in, abiding in us, becoming through obedience and action part of our very being—makes us one with Christ and fits us spiritually for touching and taking hold of God. All that is of the world passes away; he that does the will of God abides forever. Let us yield our heart and life to the words of Christ, the words in which He gives himself, the personal living Savior. Then His promises will be our rich experience: "If you abide in me, and my words abide in you, ask whatever you wish, and it shall be done for you."

Blessed Lord, today you have again revealed to me why my prayer has not been more believing and prevailing. I was more occupied with my speaking to you than your speaking to me. I had forgotten that the secret of faith in prayer is that it is in proportion to the living Word dwelling in the soul.

Your Word has taught us so clearly: "Everyone should be quick to listen, slow to speak" (James 1:19). "Do not be hasty in your heart to utter anything before God" (Ecclesiastes 5:2). Lord, teach me that it is only when your Word is appropriated into my life that my words can be embraced by you; that your Word, if it is a living power within me, will work its power with you; what your mouth has spoken, your hands will perform.

Lord, deliver me from the uncircumcised ear. Give me the opened ear of the learner, awakened morning by morning to hear the Father's voice. Even as you speak only what you hear, may my speaking be the echo of your speaking to me. "When Moses went into the tabernacle of meeting to speak with Him, he heard the voice of One speaking to him from above the mercy seat" (Numbers 7:89 NKJV). Lord, may it be so also with me. Let a life and character bearing the mark—that your words abide and are seen in it—be the preparation for the full blessing: "Ask whatever you wish, and it shall be done for you." Amen.

Chapter 23

Obedience: The Path to Power in Prayer

You did not choose me, but I chose you and appointed you to go and bear fruit—fruit that will last. Then the Father will give you whatever you ask in my name.

John 15:16

The prayer of a righteous man is powerful and effective.

James 5:16

The promise of the Father's giving whatever we ask is renewed again in a connection that shows us to whom such wonderful influence is granted. "I chose you," the Master says, "and appointed you to go and bear fruit—fruit that will last." Then He adds, "Then the Father will give you [the fruit-bearing ones] whatever you ask in my name." This is simply a fuller expression of what He said in John 15:7: "If you abide in me . . ." He described the object of this abiding as bearing "fruit" (v. 4), being "more fruitful" (v. 2), and bearing "much fruit" (v. 8): in this was God to be glorified and the mark of discipleship seen. So it appears that the "qualification" for obtaining what we ask for in prayer is to be people who bear fruit as a result of our abiding in Christ. Entire consecration to the fulfillment of our calling is the condition of effective prayer and the key to the unlimited blessings of Christ's prayer-promises.

Some Christians question whether such a statement is at variance with the doctrine of free grace. Look at the words in 1 John 3:18, 22: "Let us not love with words or tongue but with actions and in truth; if our hearts do not condemn us, we have confidence before God and receive from him anything we ask, *because* we obey his commands and do what pleases him." Also note the James text: "The prayer of a *righteous* man is powerful and effective"; that is, a man of whom it can be said, "He who does what is right is righteous, just as he is righteous" (1 John 3:7).

Notice the spirit of so many of the psalms with their confident appeal to the integrity and righteousness of the supplicant. In Psalm 18, David says, "The Lord has dealt with me according to my righteousness; according to the cleanness of my hands he has rewarded me. . . . I have been blameless before him and have kept myself from sin. The Lord has rewarded me according to my righteousness" (vv. 20, 23–24). (See also Psalms 7:8–9; 15:1–2; 17:3, 6; 26:1–6; 119:121, 153.) If we carefully consider such utterances in the light of the New Testament, we will find them to be in perfect harmony with the explicit teaching of the Savior's parting words: "If you *obey* my commands, you will remain in my love" (John 15:10); "You are my friends *if you do* what I command" (John 15:14). The word is indeed meant literally: "I chose you and appointed you to go and bear fruit. . . . *Then* the Father will give you whatever you ask in my name" (John 15:16).

Let us seek to enter into the spirit of what the Savior is teaching here. There is a danger in evangelical circles of looking one-sidedly at this experience of obtaining things by prayer and faith. Another side that God's Word puts very strongly is that obedience is the only path to blessing. We need to realize that in our relationship to God, who has created and redeemed us, our first posture ought to be that of subjection. The surrender to His supremacy, His glory, His will, His pleasure, ought to be the first and uppermost thought in our mind. The question is not how we are to obtain and enjoy His favor, for the motivation here may still be self. But rather what does God rightfully claim of us—and is infinitely and unspeakably worthy of: that His glory and pleasure should be our one object. Service and obedience were the thoughts uppermost in the mind of the Son when He dwelt on earth. Service and obedience must also be the chief objects of our desire and aim.

Notice what a prominent place the Master gives obedience, not only in this fifteenth chapter in connection with abiding but also in the fourteenth, where He speaks of the indwelling of the triune God. Verse 15 says, "If you love me, you will *obey what I command* ... and he [the Father] will give you another Counselor" (John 14:15–16). Then verse 21: "Whoever has *my commands and obeys them*, he is the one who loves me" (John 14:21); and he shall have the special love of my Father resting on him, and the special manifestation of myself. Then verse 23 gives one of the highest of all the exceedingly great and precious promises: "If anyone loves me, *he will obey my teaching*. My Father will love him, and we will come to him and make our home with him" (John 14:23). Could words put it more clearly that obedience is the way to the indwelling of the Spirit, to His revealing the

Son within us, and to His preparing us to be the abode of the Father?

The indwelling of the triune God is the heritage of those who obey Him. Obedience and faith are but two aspects of one act—surrender to God and His will. As faith is strengthened for obedience, it is in turn strengthened by it. Faith is made perfect by works. Too often our efforts to believe have been unavailing because we have not taken up the only position in which strong faith is legitimate or possible—that of entire surrender to the honor and the will of God. The man who is entirely consecrated to God and His will will find power to claim everything God has promised to him.

The application of this in prayer is very simple but also very serious: "I chose you," the Master says, "and appointed you to go and bear fruit" (John 15:16), much fruit (vv. 5, 8); "fruit that will last" (v. 16) that your life might be one of abiding fruit and abiding fruitfulness. "Then," as fruitful branches abiding in me, "the Father will give you whatever you ask in my name" (v. 16). How often we have prayed for grace to bear fruit and then wondered when the answer did not come. It was because we were reversing the Master's order. We wanted to have the comfort and the joy and the strength first that we might do the work easily without any difficulty or self-sacrifice. Only He wanted us in faith—without asking whether we felt weak or strong, whether the work was hard or easy—to simply do what He said. The path of fruit-bearing would have led us to the place and the power of prevailing prayer.

Obedience is the only path that leads to the glory of God. Not obedience instead of faith or obedience to supply the shortcomings of faith. Faith's obedience gives access to all the blessings God has for us. The baptism of the Spirit (John

14:16), the manifestation of the Son (14:21), the indwelling of the Father (14:23), the abiding in Christ's love (15:10), the privilege of His holy friendship (15:14), and the power of all-prevailing prayer (15:16)—all await the obedient.

What have we learned? We know now why we have not had power to prevail in prayer. Our life has not been as it should be. Simple, sincere obedience and abiding fruitfulness have not been its identifying marks. But with our whole heart we approve of the divine appointment: Those to whom God gives such influence in the rule of the world that at their request He will do what otherwise would not have been done are those who have learned obedience, those whose loyalty and submission to authority is above reproof. Our soul approves of the law that says obedience and fruit bearing are the path to effective prayer. With shame we acknowledge how little our lives have borne this mark.

Let us yield ourselves to accept and fulfill the appointment the Savior gives. Let us study His relationship to us as Master. With each new day may we no longer think first of comfort or joy or even blessing. Let our first thought be that we belong to the Master. Every moment and in every action we must behave as His property, as those who only seek to know and do His will. A servant, a slave of Jesus Christ—let this be the spirit that motivates me. If He says, "I no longer call you servants . . . instead I have called you friends" (John 15:15), let us accept the place of friends. "You are my friends if you do what I command" (v. 14).

The one thing He commands us as His branches is to bear fruit. We are to live to bless others, to testify of the life and the love there is in Jesus. In faith and obedience let us give our whole life to that which Jesus chose us for and appointed us —bearing fruit. As we think of His electing us to this and take up our appointment as coming from Him who always gives strength for all He commands, we will grow strong in the confidence that a life of abounding and abiding fruit bearing is within our reach. It is for the man who in obedience to Christ proves that he is doing what his Lord wills that the Father will do whatever he asks. "We have confidence before God and receive from him anything we ask, because we obey his commands and do what pleases him" (1 John 3:22).

Blessed Master, teach me to understand fully that it is only through the will of God, accepted and acted out in obedience to His commands, that we obtain power in prayer. Teach me that the path to bearing fruit is deeper growth of the branch into the Vine, and that by it we attain to that perfect oneness with you in which we may ask whatever we will.

Lord, reveal to us how together with the hosts of heaven and all the men of faith who have gone before us we may glorify you on this earth. Obedience to God is our highest privilege, because it gives access to oneness with Him and His perfect will. Reveal to us how in keeping your commandments and bearing fruit according to your will, our spiritual nature will grow up to the full stature of the perfect man, with power to ask and to receive whatever we desire.

Lord Jesus, make real to us your purpose and your power to make these promises the daily experience of all who utterly yield themselves to you. Amen.

Chapter 24

The All-Prevailing Plea

And I will do whatever you ask in my name. . . . You may ask
me for anything in my name, and I will do it. . . . Then the
Father will give you whatever you ask in my name. . . . I tell
you the truth, my Father will give you whatever you ask in my
name. Until now you have not asked for anything in my name.
Ask and you will receive. . . . In that day
you will ask in my name.

John 14:13–14; 15:16; 16:23–24, 26

Until now the disciples had not asked in the name of Christ
nor had He ever used the expression. The nearest approach
to it was "met together in my name." Here in His parting
words, He repeats the words unceasingly in connection with
those promises of unlimited meaning: *"Whatever," "Any-*
thing," "Whatever you ask," to teach them and us that His
name is our only but all-sufficient plea. The power of prayer
and the answer depend on the right use of the name.

What is a person's name? It is that word or expression by
which the person is called or known to us. When I mention
or hear a name, it calls up before me the whole man—what
I know of him and the impression he has made on me. The

name of a king includes his honor, his power, and his kingdom. His name is the symbol of his power. And so each name of God embodies and represents some part of the glory of the unseen One. The name of Christ is the expression of all He has done and all He is and lives to do as our Mediator.

What does it mean to do something in someone's name? It is to come with the power and authority of that one, as his representative and substitute. We know how such use of another's name always presumes a common interest. No one would give another the free use of his name without first being assured that his honor and interest were as safe with that person as with himself.

And what does it mean when Jesus gives us power in His name, the free use of it, with the assurance that whatever we ask in it will be given to us? The ordinary comparison of one person giving another person, on some special occasion, the liberty to ask something in his name comes altogether short here. Jesus solemnly gives to *all* His disciples a general and unlimited power of the free use of His name at *all* times for *all* they desire. He could not do this if He did not know that He could trust us with His interests, that His honor would be safe in our hands. The free use of the name of another is always the token of great confidence and of close union. He who gives his name to another stands aside to let that person act for him. He who takes the name of another gives up his own as of no value. When I go in the name of another, I deny myself; I take not only his name but I also take who he is instead of myself and who I am.

Such a use of the name of a person may be in virtue of *a legal union*. A merchant leaving town gives his chief clerk power of attorney by which he can draw thousands of dollars in the merchant's name. The clerk does this not for himself but only in the interests of the business. Because the merchant knows and trusts him as completely devoted to his interests and business, he dares to put his name and property at his command. When the Lord Jesus went to heaven, He left His work, the management of His kingdom on earth, in the hands of His servants. He could not do otherwise than to also give them His name to draw all the supplies they needed for the due conduct of His business. And they have the spiritual power to avail themselves of the name of Jesus only to the extent to which they yield themselves to live completely for the interests and the work of the Master. The use of a name always assumes the surrender of our interests to the one whom we represent.

Such use of a name may be because of a *life union*. In the case of the merchant and his clerk, the union is temporary. But we know how oneness of life on earth gives oneness of name. A child has his father's name because he has his life-blood. Often the child of a good father is honored or helped by others for the sake of the name he bears. But this would not last long if it were found that it was only a name and that the father's character was in question. The name and the character or spirit must be in harmony. When such is the case, the child will have a double claim on his father's friends; the character secures and increases the love and esteem rendered first for the name's sake. So it is with Jesus and the believer: We are one. We have one life, one Spirit with Him, and for this reason we may come in His name. Our power in using that name, whether with God or men or demons, *depends on the measure of our spiritual life union*.

There is also the *union of love* that empowers the use of a name. When a bride becomes united to her bridegroom, she gives up her own name to be called by his, and with it she is given full right to use it. She makes purchases in his name and is not refused, even if she may have been raised in a poor home. This is because the bridegroom has chosen her for himself and counts on her to care for his interests. They are now one. The heavenly Bridegroom could do nothing less. Having loved us and made us one with himself, He could only give those who bear His name the right to come before the Father for all they need. No one who truly gives himself to live in the name of Jesus fails to receive in ever-increasing measure the spiritual capacity to ask and receive in that name whatever he desires. The bearing of the name of another supposes my having given up my own name and my own independent life; but it shows just as surely my possession of all there is behind the name I have taken.

Some illustrations show us how far short the common view falls, ones that picture a messenger sent to ask in the name of another, or a guilty one appealing to the name of a guardian. But Jesus himself is with the Father. It is not an absent one in whose name we come. Even when we pray to Jesus himself, it must be in His name. The name represents the person. To ask in the name is to ask in full union of interest and life and love with Him, as one who lives in and for Him. Let the name of Jesus have undivided supremacy in my heart and life and my faith will grow in assurance that what I ask in that name cannot be refused. The name and power to ask go together. When the name of Jesus has become the power that rules my life, then its power in prayer with God will be evident.

So we see that everything depends on our relationship to the name. The power it has on my life is the power it will have in my prayers. More than one expression in Scripture clarifies this. When it says, "Do it all in the name of the Lord

Jesus" (Colossians 3:14), we see its counterpart in "Ask all." To do all and to ask all in His name go together. When we read, "We shall walk in the name of our God," we see how the power of the name must rule in the whole life. Only then will it have power in prayer. God looks not to the lips but to the life to see what the name means to us. When Scripture speaks of "men who have given their lives for the name of the Lord Jesus" or of one "ready to die for the name of the Lord Jesus," we see what our relationship to the name must be. When it is everything to me, it will obtain everything for me. If I let it have all I have, it will let me have all it has.

"I will do *whatever* you ask in my name" (John 14:13). Jesus means this literally. Christians have tried to limit it. It looks too "free." It is hardly safe to trust man so unconditionally. We do not understand that the words "in my name" are its own safeguard. It is a spiritual power that no one can use further than he has the capacity for by his living and acting in that name. As we bear that name before men, we have power to use it before God. Plead for God's Holy Spirit to show you what the name means and what the right use of it is. Through the Spirit, that name that is above every name will reign supreme in your heart and life.

Followers of Jesus, let these lessons sink deeply into your hearts. The Master says, Pray in my name; whatever you ask will be given you. Heaven is opened to you; the treasures and powers of the spiritual world are placed at your disposal on behalf of those in need around you. So let us learn to pray in the name of Jesus. As He said to His disciples, He says also to us: "Until now you have not asked for anything in my name. Ask and you will receive" (John 16:24). Let each disciple of Jesus avail himself of the rights of his royal priesthood and use the power placed at his disposal for his family and his work. Let Christians wake up and hear the message: Your prayer can obtain what otherwise would be withheld, and it can accomplish what otherwise would remain undone. Use the name of Jesus to open the treasures of heaven for this perishing world. Learn as the servants of the King to use His name: "And I will do whatever you ask in my name."

The following excerpt is adapted from *The Lord's Prayer* by A. Saphir (no publication data available).

What is meant by praying in Christ's name? It cannot mean simply appearing before God with faith in the mediation of the Savior. When the disciples asked Jesus to teach them to pray, He supplied them with petitions. And afterward Jesus said to them, "Until now you have asked nothing in my name." Until the Spirit came, the seven petitions of the Lord's Prayer lay as it were dormant within them. When by the Holy Spirit Christ descended into their hearts, they desired the blessings that Christ as our High Priest obtains for us through His prayers to the Father. And such petitions are always answered. The Father is always willing to give what Christ asks. The Spirit of Christ always teaches and influences us to offer the petitions that Christ ratifies and presents to the Father. To pray in Christ's name is therefore to be identified with Christ as our righteousness and to be identified with Him in our desires by the indwelling of the Holy Spirit. To pray *in the Spirit*, to pray *according to the will of the Father*, to pray *in Christ's name*, are identical expressions. The Father himself loves us and is willing to hear us. Two intercessors: Christ the Advocate above and the Holy Spirit the Advocate within are the gifts of His love.

This view may appear at first less consoling than a more prevalent one, which refers prayer in Christ's name chiefly to our trust in Christ's merit. The defect of this opinion is that it does not combine the intercession of the Savior with the will of the Father, and the indwelling Spirit's aid in prayer. Nor does it fully realize the mediation of Christ; for the mediation consists not merely in that for Christ's sake the Father is able to regard me and my prayer, but also in that Christ himself presents my petitions as His petitions, desired by Him for me, even as all blessings are purchased for me by His precious blood.

In all prayer, the one essential condition is that we are able to offer it in the name of Jesus, as according to His desire for us, according to the Father's will, and according to the Spirit's teaching. Thus praying in Christ's name is impossible without self-examination, without reflection, without self-denial; in short, without the aid of the Spirit.

Blessed Lord, it seems as if each lesson you give me has such fullness and depth of meaning that I think if I can only learn that one, I will truly know how to pray. Again I feel as if I need only one prayer: Lord, teach me what it is to pray in your name. Teach me to live and act, to walk and speak, to do all in the name of Jesus, that my prayer will be only in and for that blessed name.

Teach me, Lord, to hold fast the precious promise that whatever we ask for in your name, you will do and the Father will give. Though I do not yet fully understand, and still less have fully attained the wonderful union you mean when you say, "in my name," I would still cling to the promise until it fills my heart with the undoubting assurance: Anything I ask in the name of Jesus.

Lord, let your Holy Spirit teach me this. You called Him "the Comforter, whom the Father will send in my name." He knows what it is to be sent from heaven in your name, to reveal and to honor the power of that name in your servants, to use that name alone, and so to glorify you. Lord Jesus, let your Spirit dwell in me and fill me. I would and I do yield my whole being to His rule and leading. Your name and your Spirit are one; through Him your name will be the strength of my life and my prayer. Then I will be able for your name's sake to forsake all, in your name to speak to men and to God, and to prove that this is indeed the name above every name.

Lord Jesus, teach me by your Holy Spirit to pray in your name. Amen.

Chapter 25

The Holy Spirit and Prayer

In that day you will no longer ask me anything. I tell you the truth, my Father will give you whatever you ask in my name. Until now you have not asked for anything in my name. Ask and you will receive and your joy will be complete. In that day you will ask in my name. I am not saying that I will ask the Father on your behalf. No, the Father himself loves you.

John 16:23–24, 26–27

Pray in the Holy Spirit. Keep yourselves in God's love.

Jude 20–21

The words in 1 John 2:12–14 to little children, to young men, and to fathers, suggest the thought that often in the Christian life there are three great stages of experience. The first is that of the newborn child with the assurances and the joy of forgiveness. The second is the transition stage of struggle and growth in knowledge and strength: young men growing strong, God's Word doing its work in them and giving them victory over the Evil One. And then there is the final stage of maturity: the fathers who have entered deeply into the knowledge and fellowship of the eternal One.

In Christ's teaching on prayer there appear to be three stages in the prayer life, somewhat analogous.

In the Sermon on the Mount we have the initial stage: His teaching is comprised in one word, *Father.* Pray to your Father. Your Father sees, hears, knows, and will reward you—much more than any earthly father! Only be childlike and trustful.

Later on comes something like the transition stage of conflict and conquest, in words like these: "However, this kind does not go out except by prayer and fasting" (Matthew 17:21 NKJV); "And will not God bring about justice for his chosen ones, who cry out to him day and night?" (Luke 18:7).

Then we have a higher stage referred to in His parting words. The children have become men. They are now the Master's friends from whom He has no secrets and to whom He says, "Everything that I learned from my Father I have made known to you" (John 15:15); and to whom in the oft-repeated "whatever you wish" He hands over the keys to the kingdom. Now the time has come for the power of prayer in His name to be proven.

The contrast between this final stage and the previous preparatory ones our Savior marks distinctly in the words we are to meditate on: "*Until now* you have not asked for anything in my name" (John 16:24); "*In that day* you will ask in my name" (John 16:26). We know what "in that day" means. It is the day of the outpouring of the Holy Spirit. The great work Christ was to do on the cross, the mighty power and the complete victory to be manifested in His resurrection and ascension, were to lead to the coming down from heaven, as never before, of the glory of God to dwell in men. The Spirit of the glorified Jesus was to come and be the life of His disciples. And one of the marks of that wonderful spirit dispensation was to be a power in prayer hitherto unknown—prayer in the name of Jesus, asking and obtaining whatever they wished to manifest the reality of the Spirit's indwelling.

To understand how the coming of the Holy Spirit was indeed to begin a new epoch in the prayer-world, we must remember who He is, what His work is, and the significance of His not being given until Jesus was glorified. It is in the Spirit that God exists, for He is Spirit. It is in the Spirit that the Son was begotten of the Father. It is in the fellowship of the Spirit that the Father and the Son are one. The eternal, never-ending giving to the Son that is the Father's prerogative, and the eternal asking and receiving that is the Son's right and blessedness—it is through the Spirit that this communion of life and love is maintained. It has been so from all eternity. It is especially so now, when the Son as Mediator ever lives to pray. The great work of reconciling in His own body God and man that Jesus began on earth, He carries on in heaven. To accomplish this He took up in His own person the conflict between God's righteousness and our sin. In His own body on the cross He once for all ended the struggle. Then He ascended to heaven that from there He might in each member of His body carry out the deliverance and manifest the victory He had obtained. To do this, He ever lives to pray. And in His unceasing intercession, He places himself in living fellowship with the unceasing prayer of His redeemed ones. It is His intercession that shows itself in their prayers and gives them power that they never had before.

All this is done through the Holy Spirit. The Holy Spirit

is the Spirit of the glorified Jesus, given after Jesus had been glorified (John 7:39). This gift of the Father was something distinctively new, entirely different from what Old Testament saints had known. The work that the blood effected in heaven when Christ entered within the veil was something new. The redemption of our human nature into fellowship with His resurrection power and His exaltation glory was so intensely real, the taking up of our humanity in Christ into the life of the triune God was an event of such inconceivable significance that the Holy Spirit, who had to come from Christ's exalted humanity to testify in our hearts of what Christ had accomplished, was no longer as He had been in the Old Testament. He came first as the Spirit of the glorified Jesus. The Son, who from eternity was God, had entered upon a new existence as man and returned to heaven with what He did not have before. So the blessed Spirit, whom the Son on His ascension received from the Father into His glorified humanity (Acts 2:33), also came to us with a new life not previously His to communicate. Under the Old Testament He was invoked as the Spirit of God. At Pentecost He descended as the Spirit of the glorified Jesus, bringing down and communicating to us the full fruit and power of the accomplished redemption.

In the intercession of Christ, the continued efficacy and application of His redemption is maintained. Through the Holy Spirit descending from Christ to us, we are drawn up into the great stream of His ever-ascending prayers. The Spirit prays for us without words. In the depths of a heart where even thoughts are at times formless, the Spirit takes us up into the wonderful flow of the life of the triune God. Through the Spirit, Christ's prayers become ours, and ours are made His; we ask what we will and it is given to us. We then understand from experience, "Until now you have not asked for anything in my name. . . . *In that day* you will ask in my name" (John 16:24, 26).

What we need to pray for in the name of Christ and ask that we may receive that our joy may be full is the baptism of the Holy Spirit. This is more than the Spirit of God under the Old Testament. This is more than the Spirit of conversion and regeneration that the disciples had before Pentecost. This is more than the Spirit with a *measure* of His influence and working. This is the Holy Spirit, the Spirit of the glorified Jesus in His exaltation power, coming on us as the Spirit of the indwelling Jesus, revealing the Son and the Father within (John 14:16–23). When this Spirit is the Spirit not only of our hours of prayer but also of our whole life and walk; when this Spirit glorifies Jesus in us by revealing the completeness of His work, making us wholly one with Him and like Him; then we can pray in His name, because we are indeed one with Him. Then it is that we have that instant access to the Father to which Jesus referred: "In that day you will ask in my name. I am not saying that I will ask the Father on your behalf" (John 16:26).

How we need to understand and believe that to be filled with this Spirit of the glorified One is the one need of God's believing people! Then we will understand "and pray in the Spirit on all occasions with all kinds of prayers and requests" (Ephesians 6:18), and "pray in the Holy Spirit" (Jude 1:20).

Once again we see that what our prayer avails depends upon what we are and what our life is. Living in the name of Christ is the secret of praying in His name. Living in the Spirit fits one for praying in the Spirit. Abiding in Christ gives the right and the power to ask what we will. The extent of the abiding is the exact measure of the power in prayer.

The Spirit dwelling within us prays, not in words and thoughts always, but in a breath deeper than utterance. There is real prayer according to how much there is of Christ's Spirit in us. If our lives are full of Christ and full of His Spirit, the wonderfully unlimited answers to our prayers will no longer be rare or unusual. "In that day you will no longer ask me anything. I tell you the truth, my Father will give you whatever you ask in my name. Until now you have not asked for anything in my name. Ask and you will receive, and your joy will be complete. In that day you will ask in my name. I am not saying that I will ask the Father on your behalf" (John 16:23–24, 26).

Prayer has often been compared to breathing: we have only to carry out the comparison fully to see how wonderful the place is that the Holy Spirit occupies. With every breath we expel the impure air that would soon cause our death, and inhale again the fresh air to which we owe our life. So we exhale the sins in confession and the needs and the desires of our heart in prayer. Drawing in our breath again, we inhale the fresh air of the promises, the love and the life of God in Christ. We do this through the Holy Spirit, who is the breath of life.

The Father breathes the Spirit into us to unite Him with our spirit. God draws in again His breath, and the Spirit returns to Him laden with the desires and needs of our hearts. Thus the Holy Spirit is the breath of the life of God and the breath of the new life in us. As the Spirit of God, in whom the Father and the Son are one, and the intercession of the Son reaches the Father, He is to us the Spirit of prayer. True prayer is the living experience of the truth of the holy Trinity. The Spirit's breathing, the Son's intercession, the Father's will—these three become one in us.

In holy awe I bow before you, the triune God. Again I have seen how the mystery of prayer is the mystery of the holy Trinity. I adore the Father who ever hears, the Son who ever lives to pray, and the Holy Spirit, proceeding from the Father and the Son, to lift us up into the fellowship of that ever-blessed, never-ceasing place of prayer. I bow, my God, in adoring worship before this infinite condescension that through the Holy Spirit takes us into the divine life and fellowship of love.

Blessed Lord Jesus, teach me to understand that it is the indwelling Spirit flowing from you and uniting to you who is the Spirit of prayer. Teach me what it is as an empty, wholly consecrated vessel, to yield myself to Him as my life. Teach me to honor and trust Him as a living person to lead my life and my prayers. Teach me to wait in holy silence in prayer and give Him place to breathe within me His unutterable intercession. Teach me that through Him it is possible to pray without ceasing—to pray without failing—because He makes me a partaker of the never-ceasing and never-failing intercession in which you, the Son, appear before the Father. Lord, fulfill in me your promise "In that day you will ask in my name. I tell you the truth, my Father will give you whatever you ask in my name." Amen.

Chapter 26

Christ the Intercessor

But I have prayed for you ... that your faith may not fail.

Luke 22:32

I am not saying that I will ask the Father on your behalf.

John 16:26

He always lives to intercede.

Hebrews 7:25

All growth in the spiritual life is connected with a clearer insight into what Jesus is to us. The more I realize that Christ must be all to me and in me and that all in Christ is for me, the more I learn to live the true life of faith, which in dying to self lives wholly in Christ. The Christian life is no longer the vain struggle to live right, but resting in Christ and finding strength in Him as our life, to fight the fight and gain the victory of faith. This is especially true of the life of prayer. As it too comes under the law of faith alone and is seen in the light of the fullness and completeness there is in Jesus, the believer understands that it need no longer be a matter of strain or anxious care but an experience of what Christ will do for him and in him. Further, it will be a participation in that life of Christ that on earth as in heaven ever ascends to the Father as prayer. He begins to pray not only trusting in the merits of Jesus or in the intercession by which our unworthy prayers are made acceptable but also in that close union by which He prays in us and we in Him.* The whole of salvation is Christ himself. He has given himself to us. He lives in us. Because He prays, we also pray. Just as the disciples, when they saw Jesus pray, asked Him to make them partakers of what He knew of prayer, so we, seeing Him as intercessor on the throne, know that He makes us participate with Him in the life of prayer.

How clearly this comes out in the last night of His life. In His high-priestly prayer (John 17), He shows us how and what He has to pray to the Father and will pray when once ascended to heaven. But in His parting address He repeatedly connected His going to the Father with *their* new life of prayer. The two would be ultimately connected. His entrance into the work of His eternal intercession would be the commencement and the power of their new prayer life in His name. It is the sight of Jesus in His intercession that gives us power to pray in His name. All right and power of prayer is Christ's. He makes us share in His intercession.

To understand this, think first of His intercession. He ever lives to make intercession for us. The work of Christ on earth as Priest was but a beginning. It was as Aaron He shed His blood. It is as Melchizedek that He now lives within the

---

*See the difference between having Christ as Advocate or Intercessor who stands outside of us and having Him within us—our abiding in Him and He in us through the Holy Spirit—perfecting our union with Him so that we can go directly to the Father in His name (Beck of Tubingen).

veil to continue His work after the power of eternal life. As Melchizedek He is more glorious than Aaron, so it is in the work of intercession that the atonement has its true power and glory. "Christ Jesus, who died—*more than that, who . . .* is at the right hand of God and is also interceding for us" (Romans 8:34). That intercession is an intense reality, a work that is absolutely necessary and without which the continued application of redemption cannot take place.

In the incarnation and resurrection of Jesus the wonderful reconciliation took place by which man became partaker of the divine life and blessedness. But the real personal appropriation of this reconciliation in each of His members here below cannot take place without the unceasing exercise of His divine power by the head in heaven. In all conversion and sanctification, in every victory over sin and the world, there is a flowing forth of the power of Him who is mighty to save. This exercise of His power only takes place through His prayer. He asks of the Father and receives from the Father. "*He is able* to save completely . . . *because* he always lives to intercede" (Hebrews 7:25). There is never a need of His people without His receiving in intercession what the Godhead has to give. His mediation on the throne is as real and indispensable as on the cross. Nothing takes place without His intercession. It engages all His time and powers. It is His unceasing occupation at the right hand of the Father.

We participate not only in the benefits of His work but also in the work itself, because we are His body. Body and members are one. "The head cannot say to the feet, I don't need you!" (1 Corinthians 12:21). We share with Jesus in all He is and has. "I have given them the glory that you gave me" (John 17:22). We are partakers of His life, His righteousness, His work; we share with Him in His intercession too; it is not a work He does without us.

We do this because we are partakers of His life. Christ is our life; "I no longer live, but Christ lives in me" (Galatians 2:20). The life in Him and in us is identical, one and the same. His life in heaven is a life of never-ending prayer. When it descends and takes possession of us, it does not lose its character. In us too it is the ceaseless life of prayer—a life that without ceasing asks and receives from God. It is not as if there were two separate currents of prayer rising upward, one from Him and one from His people. The substantial life-union is also a prayer-union: what He prays passes through us and what we pray passes through Him. He is the angel with the golden censer: "He was given much incense to offer, with the prayers of all the saints, on the golden altar before the throne" (Revelation 8:3).

The Only-begotten is the only one who has the right to pray. To Him alone it was said, "Ask, and it shall be given you." As in all other things the fullness dwells in Him, as does the true prayerfulness; He alone has the power of prayer. Just as growth in our spiritual life involves a clearer insight into the fact that all the treasures are *in Him* and that we too are *in Him*, so it is with our prayer life. Our faith in the intercession of Jesus must not only be that He prays in our place when we do not or cannot pray, but that as the Author of our life and our faith He leads us to pray in unison with himself. Our prayer must be a work of faith in this sense also. Just as Jesus communicates His whole life to us, He also out of that prayerfulness that is His alone breathes into us our prayers.

To many believers it was a new epoch in their spiritual lives when it was revealed to them how truly and entirely Christ was their life, standing as the guarantee for their remaining faithful and obedient. It was then that he first began to truly live a *faith-life*. No less blessed will be the discovery that Christ is the guarantee for our prayer life, the center and embodiment of all prayer, to be communicated by Him through the Holy Spirit to His people.

"He always lives to intercede" (Hebrews 7:25) as the Head of the body, as the Leader in that new and living way that He has opened up, as Author and Perfecter of our faith. He provides everything for the life of His redeemed ones by giving His own life to them. He cares for their life of prayer by taking them up into His heavenly prayer life, by giving and maintaining His prayer life within them. "I have prayed for you" not to render our faith needless, but "that your faith may not fail" (Luke 22:32). Our faith and prayer of faith is rooted in His. It is "If you abide in me" (John 15:7), the ever-living Intercessor, and pray with me and in me, "Ask whatever you wish, and it will be given you" (John 15:7).

The thought of our fellowship in the intercession of Jesus reminds us of what He taught us more than once before: how all these wonderful prayer promises have as their aim and their justification the glory of God in the manifestation of His kingdom and the salvation of sinners. As long as we only or mainly pray for ourselves, the promises of the Savior's last night must remain a sealed book to us. It is to the fruit-bearing branches of the Vine; to disciples sent into the world as the Father sent Him, to live for perishing men; it is to His faithful servants and intimate friends who take up the work He left behind, who like their Lord have become as seed corn, losing their life in order to multiply—to such the promises are given. Let us each find out what the work is and which souls are entrusted to our special prayers. Let us make our intercession for them our life of fellowship with

God, and we shall not only find the promises of power in prayer proven true to us but we shall also see how our abiding in Christ and His abiding in us make us share in His own joy of blessing and saving men.

How wonderful is this intercession of our blessed Lord Jesus, to which we not only owe everything but in which we are also taken up as active partners and fellow workers! Now we understand what it is to pray in the name of Jesus and why it has such power—in His name, in His Spirit, and in perfect union with Him. This wonderful, ever-active, and most efficacious intercession of the man Christ Jesus—when shall we be wholly caught up into it and always pray in it?

The following excerpt is adapted from Dr. I. T. Beck's *Christliche Ethik* (no publication data available).

> The new epoch of prayer in the name of Jesus is pointed out by Christ as the time of the outpouring of the Spirit, in which the disciples enter upon a more enlightened apprehension of the economy of redemption and become as clearly conscious of their oneness with Jesus as of His oneness with the Father. Their prayer in the name of Jesus is now directed to the Father himself. Jesus says that while He had previously spoken of the time before the Spirit's coming—"I will pray the Father, and he will give you the Comforter"—this prayer has as its central thought our being united to God in Christ. Jesus Christ must have been revealed to us not only through the truth in the mind but also in our inmost personal consciousness as the living personal reconciliation, as He in whom God's fatherhood and Father-love have been perfectly united with human nature and it with God. Not that with the immediate prayer to the Father the mediatorship of Christ is set aside, but it is no longer looked at as something external, existing outside of us, but as a real, living spiritual existence within

us, so that the Christ *for us*, the Mediator, has really become Christ *in us*.

When the consciousness of this oneness between God in Christ and us in Christ still is waning, or has been darkened by the sense of guilt, then the prayer of faith looks to our Lord as the Advocate, who prays to the Father *for us*. (Compare John 16:26 with 14:16–17; 9:20; Luke 22:32; 1 John 2:1.) To take Christ thus in prayer as Advocate is according to John 16:26 not the same as prayer in His name.

Christ's advocacy is meant to lead us on to that inner self-standing life-union with Him, and with the Father in Him, in virtue of which Christ is He in whom God enters into immediate relationship and unites himself with us, and in whom we in all circumstances enter into immediate relationship with God. Even so the prayer in the name of Jesus does not consist in our prayer at His command: the disciples had prayed thus ever since the Lord had given them His "Our Father," and yet He says, "Hitherto ye have not prayed in my name." Only when the mediation of Christ has become, through the indwelling of the Holy Spirit, life and power within us, so that His mind has taken possession of and filled our personal consciousness and will, only then His name is become truth and power in us and we have in the name of Jesus the free, direct access to the Father and the certainty of being heard.

Prayer in the name of Jesus is the liberty of a son with the Father, just as Jesus had this freedom as the first and only begotten Son. We pray in the place of Jesus not as if we could put ourselves in His place but insofar as we are in Him and He in us. We go directly to the Father, but only as the Father is in Christ, not as if He were separate from Christ. Wherever the inner man does not live in Christ and He is not present as the living One, where His Word is not ruling in the heart in its Spirit-power, where His truth and life have not become the life of our soul, it is vain to think that a formula like "for the sake of thy dear Son" will avail anything.

Blessed Lord, in adoration I would again bow before you. Your whole redemptive work has now passed into prayer. All that now occupies you in maintaining and dispensing what you purchased with your blood is only prayer. You ever live to pray. Because we abide in you, direct access to the Father is always open. Our life can be one of unceasing prayer. The answer to our prayer is assured.

Blessed Lord, you have invited your people to be your fellow workers in a life of prayer. You have united yourself with your people and make them as your body share with you in that ministry of intercession through which alone the world can be filled with the fruit of your redemption and the glory of the Father. With more liberty than ever I come to you, my Lord, and beseech you: Teach me to pray. Your life is prayer; your life is mine. Teach me to pray like you.

Lord, help me to realize afresh that you are in the Father, I am in you, and you are in me. Let the uniting power of the Holy Spirit make my whole life abide in yours and your intercession, so that my prayer may be its echo. Lord Jesus, let your mind in everything be in me, and my life in everything be in you. So will I be prepared to be the channel through which your intercession pours its blessing into the world. Amen.

Chapter 27

Christ the High Priest

Father, I want those you have given me to be
with me where I am.

John 17:24

In His parting address, Jesus gives His disciples the full revelation of what the new life was to be when once the kingdom of God had come in power. In the indwelling of the Holy Spirit, in union with Him, the heavenly Vine, in their going forth to witness and to suffer for Him, they were to find their calling and their blessedness. In between His telling of their future new life, the Lord had repeatedly given the most unlimited promises as to the power their prayers might have.

In closing, He himself proceeds to pray. To let His disciples have the joy of knowing what His intercession for them in heaven as their High Priest will be, He gives this precious legacy of His prayer to the Father. He does this at the same time because they as priests are to share in His work of intercession that they and we might know how to perform this holy work. In the teaching of our Lord on this last night, we have learned to understand that these astonishing prayer-promises have not been given on our own behalf but in the interest of the Lord and His kingdom. From the Lord alone can we learn what the prayer in His name is to be and what it is to obtain. We have seen that to pray in His name is to pray in perfect unity with Him. The high-priestly prayer will teach all that prayer in the name of Jesus may ask and expect to receive.

This prayer is ordinarily divided into three parts. Our Lord first prays for himself (John 17:1–5), then for His disciples (vv. 6–19), and last for all the believing people through all ages (vv. 20–26). The follower of Jesus who dedicates himself to the work of intercession and wants to pray down blessing upon his circle in the name of Jesus, will submit humbly to the guidance of the Spirit and study this wonderful prayer as one of the most important prayer lessons.

First, Jesus prays for himself to be glorified so that He may glorify the Father. "Father . . . glorify your Son. . . . And now, Father, glorify me" (John 17:1, 5). He shows the grounds on which He prays. A holy covenant had been concluded between the Father and the Son in heaven. The Father had promised Him power over all flesh as the reward of His work. He had done the work, He had glorified the Father, and His one purpose is now to glorify Him further. With utmost boldness He asks that the Father may glorify Him that He may now be and do for His people all He has undertaken.

You who would follow Jesus, here is the first lesson in your work of priestly intercession to be learned from the example of your great High Priest: To pray in the name of Jesus is to pray in unity and in sympathy with Him. The Son began His prayer by making clear His relationship to the Father, pleading His work and obedience and His desire to see the Father glorified. We must do the same. Draw near and appear before the Father in Christ. Plead His finished work. Say that you are one with it, you trust in it, and you live by it. Say that you too have given yourself to finish the work the Father has given you to do and to live alone for His glory. Then confidently ask that the Son may be glorified in you.

This is praying in the name, in the very words, in the Spirit of Jesus, in union with Jesus himself. Such prayer has power. If with Jesus you glorify the Father, the Father will glorify Jesus by doing what you ask in His name. It is only when your own personal relationship on this point, like Christ's, is clear with God, when you are glorifying Him and seeking all for His glory so that, like Christ, you will have power to intercede for those around you.

Our Lord next prays for the circle of His disciples. He speaks of them as those whom the Father has given Him. Their distinguishing mark is that they have received Christ's word. He says of them that He now sends them into the world in His place, just as the Father has sent Him. He asks two things for them: that the Father will keep them from the Evil One and that He will sanctify them through His Word, because He sanctifies himself for them.

Just like the Lord, each believing intercessor has his own immediate circle for whom he first prays. Parents have their children, teachers their pupils, pastors their flocks, all workers their special charge, all believers those whose care lies upon their hearts. It is essential that intercession should be personal, pointed, and definite. Our first prayer must always be that they may receive the Word. But this prayer will not avail unless with our Lord we say, "I have given them your word" (John 17:14). This gives us liberty and power in intercession for souls—not only to pray for them but also to speak to them. And when they have received the Word, let us pray for their being kept from the Evil One and that they be sanctified through that Word. Instead of doubting or judging or giving up on those who fall, let us pray for our circle: "Holy Father, protect them by the power of your name" (John 17:11); "Sanctify them by the truth" (John 17:17). Prayer in the name of Jesus avails much: "Ask whatever you wish, and it will be given you" (John 15:7).

Then follows our Lord's prayer for a still wider circle: "My prayer is not for them alone. I pray also for those who will believe in me through their message" (John 17:20). His priestly heart enlarges itself to embrace all places and all time, and He prays that all who belong to Him may everywhere be one, as God's proof to the world of the divinity of His mission, and then that they may ever be with Him in His glory. Until then, "that the love you have for me may be in them and that I myself may be in them" (John 17:26).

The disciple of Jesus who has first in his own circle of responsibility proved the power of prayer, cannot confine himself to its limits. He prays for the church universal and its various branches. He prays especially for the unity of the Spirit and of love. He prays for its being one in Christ as a witness to the world that Christ, who wonderfully made love triumph over selfishness and separation, is indeed the Son of God sent from heaven. Every believer ought to pray that the unity of the church—not in external organization but in spirit and in truth—may be made known.

So much for the *matter* of prayer. Now for its style. Jesus says, "Father, I want . . ." (John 17:24). On the ground of His right as Son, the Father's promise to Him, and His finished work, He was able to ask whatever He wanted. The Father said to Him, "Ask of me, and I will give to you." He simply availed himself of the Father's promise. Jesus has given us a similar promise: "*Ask whatever you wish, and it will be given you*" (John 15:7). He asks me in His name to ask what I wish.

Abiding in Him in a living union in which man is nothing and Christ is all, the believer has the liberty to take the word of His High Priest. In answer to the question "What do you want?" he is able to say, "Father, I want all that you have promised." This is true faith. This honors God, to have the confidence to ask whatever you will and know that it is acceptable to Him. At first sight, our heart shrinks from the expression. We feel neither the liberty nor the power to speak like this. It is a word for which alone, in the most entire abnegation of our will, grace will be given, but for which grace will most assuredly be given to each one who loses his will in his Lord's. He that loses his will will find it; he that gives up his will entirely will find it again renewed and strengthened with a divine strength. "Father, I want . . ." (John 17:24): this is the keynote of the everlasting, ever-active, all-prevailing intercession of our Lord in heaven. It is only in union with Him that our prayer avails; in union with Him it avails much.

If we but abide in Him, living, and walking, and doing all things in His name; if we but come and bring each separate petition, tested and touched by His Word and Spirit, and cast it into the mighty stream of intercession that goes up from Him, to be borne upward and presented before the Father—then we shall have the full confidence that we receive the petitions we ask. The "Father, *I want* . . ." (John 17:24) will be breathed into us by the Spirit himself. We shall lose ourselves in Him and become nothing, to find that in our impotence we have power and prevail.

Disciples of Jesus, called to be like your Lord in His priestly intercession, when will we be like Him? When will we awaken to the glory—passing all conception—of our destiny to plead and prevail with God for perishing men? When will we shake off the sloth that masks itself with a pretense of humility? Let us yield ourselves wholly to God's Spirit, that He may fill our wills with light and with power, to know, to take, and to possess all that our God is waiting to give to a will that takes hold of Him.

Blessed High Priest, who am I that you should invite me to share with you in your power of prevailing intercession? Why, Lord, am I so slow to understand and believe, to exercise this wonderful privilege to which you have redeemed your people? Lord, give your grace that this may increasingly be my unceasing life-work—to pray without ceasing, to bring the blessing of heaven down on all around me here on earth.

Lord, I come to accept this as my calling. For this I would forsake all and follow you. Into your hands I would yield my whole being in believing trust. Form and train me to be one of your prayer warriors. Inspire me to be one with the wrestlers who watch and strive in prayer; Israels, God's princes, who have power and prevail. Take possession of my heart and fill it with one desire—the glory of God in the ingathering, sanctification, and union of those whom the Father has given you. Take my mind and let this be my study and my wisdom, to know when prayer can bring a blessing. Take me wholly and fit me as a priest to stand always before God and to bless in His name.

Blessed Lord, may it be here, as through all my spiritual

life: you being all and I being nothing. May it be my experience that he that has and seeks nothing for himself receives all, even to the wonderful grace of sharing with you in your everlasting ministry of intercession. Amen.

Chapter 28

Christ the Sacrifice

"Abba, Father," he said, "everything is possible for you. Take this cup from me. Yet not what I will, but what you will."

Mark 14:36

What a contrast within the space of a few hours! What a transition from the quietness of "Father, the time has come" (John 17:1) to falling on the ground and crying, "Abba, Father! . . . Take this cup from me. Yet not what I will." In the one we see the High Priest within the veil in His all-prevailing intercession; in the other, the sacrifice on the altar opening the way through the rent veil. In order of time the high priestly "Father, the time has come" precedes the sacrificial "Abba, Father! . . . Not what I will"; but this was only to show beforehand what the intercession would be when once the sacrifice was brought. In reality it was that prayer at the altar in which the prayer before the throne had its origin and its power. Because of the entire surrender of His will in Gethsemane, the High Priest on the throne had the power to ask what He would. He has the right to let His people share in that power also and ask what they will.

This Gethsemane lesson is one of the most sacred and

precious of all. To a superficial learner it may appear to take away the courage to pray in faith. If the earnest supplication of the Son's "Take this cup from me" was not heard, if He had to say, "Yet not what I will," how much more do we need to say it? Now it appears impossible that the promises the Lord had given only a few hours previously—"Whatever you ask," "Whatever you wish"—could have been meant literally. But a deeper insight into the meaning of Gethsemane teaches us that it is precisely here that we have sure ground and an open way to assurance of an answer to our prayer. Let us draw near in reverent and adoring wonder, to gaze on this great sight of God's Son offering up prayer and supplications with strong crying and tears—and not obtaining what He asks! He is our Teacher and will open up to us the mystery of His holy sacrifice as revealed in this awesome prayer.

To understand the prayer, let us note the infinite difference between what our Lord prayed a little while ago as a royal High Priest and what He begs here in His weakness. *There* He prayed for the glorifying of the Father and the glorifying of himself and His people as the fulfillment of distinct promises that had been given Him. What He asked He knew to be according to the word and the will of the Father; He might boldly say, "Father! I will." *Here* He prays for something in regard to which the Father's will is not yet clear to Him. As far as He knows, it is the Father's will that he should drink the cup. He had told His disciples of the cup He must drink. A little later He would again say, "Shall I not drink the cup the Father has given me?" (John 18:11). It was for this reason He had come to earth.

When the unutterable agony of soul burst upon Him as the power of darkness came over Him and He began to taste the first drops of death as the wrath of God against sin, His human nature shuddered in the presence of the awful reality of being made a curse. Then He cried out in anguish, desiring that if God's purpose could be accomplished without it, He might be spared the awful cup: "May this cup be taken from me" (Matthew 26:39). That desire was evidence of the intense reality of His humanity. The "Yet not as I will" kept that desire from being sinful. He pleadingly cries, "All things are possible with you," and returns again to still more earnest prayer that the cup may be removed.

His three-times-repeated "Yet not what I will" constitutes the very essence and worth of His sacrifice. He had asked for something of which He could not say, I *know* it is your will. He had pleaded God's power and love and then withdrew it in His final "Your will be done" (Matthew 26:42). The prayer that the cup should pass away could not be answered; the prayer of submission that God's will be done was heard, first in His victory over fear, and then over the power of death.

In the denial of His will and complete surrender to the will of the Father, Christ's obedience reached its highest perfection. From the sacrifice of His will in Gethsemane, the sacrifice of His life on Calvary derives its value. As Scripture says, He learned obedience here and became the author of everlasting salvation to all that obey Him. It was because He there, in that prayer, became obedient unto death, even the death of the cross, that God has highly exalted Him and given Him the power to ask what He will. It was by Christ's submission in Gethsemane to not have His will done that He secured for His people the right to "ask whatever [they] wish" (John 15:7).

Gethsemane offers deep mysteries. First, the Father offers His well-beloved the cup of wrath. Second, the Son, always obedient, shrinks back and implores that He may not have to drink it. Third, the Father does not grant the Son His request but gives the cup. Fourth, the Son yields His will, is content that His will not be done, and goes to Calvary to drink the cup. In Gethsemane I see that my Lord can give me unlimited assurance of an answer to my prayers. He won the privilege for me by His consent to have His petition unanswered.

This is in harmony with the whole scheme of redemption. Our Lord always wins for us the opposite of what He suffered. He was bound that we might go free. He was made sin that we might become the righteousness of God. He died that we might live. He bore God's curse that God's blessing might be ours. He endured not having His prayer answered that our prayers might be answered. He said, "Not as I will," that He might say to us, "If you remain in me, *ask whatever you wish*, and it will be given you" (John 15:7).

Here in Gethsemane the word "if you abide in me" acquires new force and depth. Christ is our Head, who stands in our place and bears what we must have borne forever. We deserved that God should turn a deaf ear to us and never listen to our cry. Christ comes and suffers this too for us. He suffers what we merited. For our sins He suffers beneath the burden of that unanswered prayer. But now His suffering avails for me. His merit has won for me the answer to every prayer, if I abide in Him.

I must abide in Him as He bows there in Gethsemane. As my Head, He not only once suffered for me but also ever lives in me, breathing and working His own nature into mine. The eternal Spirit, through which He offered himself unto God, is the Spirit that dwells in me too and makes me partaker of the same obedience and sacrifice of the will unto God. That Spirit teaches me to yield my will entirely to the will of the Father, to give it up even though it is not directly sinful.

The Spirit opens my ears to wait in great gentleness and teachableness of soul for what the Father has to speak and to teach day by day. He shows me how in God's will there is union with God himself. He shows me that entire surrender to God's will is the Father's claim, the Son's example, and the soul's true blessedness. He leads my will into the fellowship of Christ's death and resurrection. My will dies in Him, in Him to be made alive again. He breathes into it, a renewed and quickened will, a holy insight into God's perfect will, a holy joy in yielding itself to be an instrument of that will. He gives holy liberty and power to lay hold of God's will to answer prayer. With my whole will I learn to live for the interests of God and His kingdom, to exercise the power of that will—crucified but risen again—in nature and in prayer, on earth and in heaven, with men and with God.

The more deeply I enter into the prayer "Not what I will" of Gethsemane, and abide in Him who spoke it, the fuller is my spiritual access into the power of His "But what you will." Then the soul finds that the personal will, which has become nothing so that God's will may be done, becomes inspired with a divine strength to truly will what God wills and to claim what has been promised in the name of Christ.

Listen to Christ in Gethsemane as He calls, "If you remain in me, ask whatever you wish, and it will be given you" (John 15:7). Being of one mind and spirit with Him in His giving up everything to God's will, living as He did in obedience and surrender to the Father—this is abiding in Him. This is the secret of power in prayer.

Blessed Lord Jesus, Gethsemane was your school, where you learned to pray and to obey. It is still the school where you lead all your disciples who want to learn to obey and to pray as you do. Lord, teach me to pray in faith that you atoned for and conquered our self-will and can indeed give us grace to pray as you do.

Lamb of God, I would follow you to Gethsemane, there to become one with you and to abide in you as you, unto death, yielded up your will unto the Father. With you, through you, in you, I yield my will in absolute and entire surrender to the will of the Father. I claim in faith the power of your victory, conscious of my own weakness and the secret power with which my self-will would assert itself and again take its place on the throne. You triumphed over it and delivered me from it. In your death I would daily live. In your life I would daily die. Abiding in you through the power of your eternal Spirit, let my will be the tuned instrument that yields to every touch of the will of God. With my whole soul I say with you, "Father . . . not what I will, but what you will."

Then, blessed Lord, open my heart and the hearts of all your people to accept fully the glory of the truth that a will given up to God is a will accepted by God to be used in His service, to desire, purpose, determine, and will that which is according to God's will. Then it will be a choice that in the power of the Holy Spirit can exercise its royal prerogative in prayer, to loose and to bind in heaven and on earth, to ask whatever it wishes and to say it will be done.

Lord Jesus, teach me to pray. Amen.

Chapter 29

Our Boldness in Prayer

This is the confidence we have in approaching God: that if we
ask anything according to his will, he hears us. And if we know
that he hears us—whatever we ask—we know
that we have what we asked of him.

1 John 5:14–15

Undoubtedly one of the greatest hindrances to believing prayer is this: many do not know if what they ask agrees with the will of God. As long as they are in doubt on this point, they cannot have the boldness to ask in the assurance that they will receive. And they soon begin to think that if they have made known their requests and receive no answer, it is best to leave it to God to do according to His good pleasure. The words of John, "If we ask anything *according to his will,* he hears us" (1 John 5:14), as they understand them, make answer to prayer impossible, because they cannot be sure what the will of God is. They think of God's will as His hidden counsel. How can man fathom what may be the purpose of the all-wise God?

However, this is the very opposite of what John was aiming at. He wanted to stir us to boldness, to confidence, to full assurance of faith in prayer. He says, "*This is the confidence we have in approaching God*" (v. 14) that we can say, "Father, you know and I know that I ask according to your will. I know you hear me." "This is the confidence we have in approaching God: that if we ask anything according to his will, he hears us" (v. 14). But He adds at once, "If we know that he hears us—whatever we ask—we *know*," through this faith, "that we have what we asked of him" (v.15), that while we pray we receive "the petition," the special things we have asked of Him.

John assumes that when we pray we first find out if our prayers are according to the will of God. They may be according to God's will, and yet not be answered at once, or they may not be answered without persevering prayer. To encourage us to persevere and be strong in faith, He tells us that if we ask anything according to His will, He hears us. It is obvious that if we are uncertain about whether our petitions are according to His will, we will not have the comfort of knowing that we "have the petitions which we have asked of him."

But here is the problem. More than one believer says, "I do not know if what I desire is according to the will of God. God's will is the purpose of His infinite wisdom. It is impossible for me to know if He thinks something else is better for me than what I want, or if He has some reason for withholding what I ask." Of course, when we think like this, the prayer of faith described by Jesus does become impossible. There may be the prayer of submission and of trust in God's wisdom, but there cannot be the prayer of faith. The great mistake here is that God's children do not really believe that it is possible to know God's will. Or if they believe it, they do not take the time and trouble to find out what it is.* We will learn to know that our petitions are according to His will through God's holy Word received into the heart, life, and will, and through God's Holy Spirit, accepted in His indwelling and leading.

There is a secret or hidden will of God with which we often fear our prayers may not agree. It is not with this will but with His will as revealed in His Word that we are dealing in prayer. Our notions about what God's secret will is and how it might render the answers to our prayers impossible are usually in error. Childlike faith simply believes the Father's assurance that it is His will to hear our prayers and to do what faith in His Word desires.

The Father has revealed through general promises in His Word the great principles of His will concerning His people. The child must take the promise and apply it to the circumstances in his life to which it refers. Whatever he asks within the limits of that revealed will, he can know to be according to the will of God and he may confidently expect an answer. God's Word gives us the revelation of His will and plans for us, for all His people, and for the world. He also gives us precious promises of grace and power by which He will carry out His plans and do His work among and through His people.

As faith becomes strong and bold enough to claim the fulfillment of the promise in a particular case, we have the assurance that our prayers are heard and that they are according to God's will. As an illustration, take the words of John in the verse following our text: "If anyone sees his brother commit a sin that does not lead to death, he should

---

*See this illustrated in the extracts from George Müller in the appendix at the end of this book.

pray and God will give him life" (1 John 5:16). Such is the general promise; and the believer who pleads on the ground of this promise prays according to the will of God.

But this comprehension of God's will is something spiritual, and must be spiritually discerned. It is not a matter of logic that we can argue out: God has said it; I will have it. Nor has every Christian the same gift or calling. While the general will revealed in the promise is the same for all, there is for each one a different special will according to God's purpose. Herein is the wisdom of the saints, to know this special will of God for each of us according to the measure of grace given us. Then we ask in prayer just what God has prepared and made possible for each. It is to communicate this wisdom that the Holy Spirit dwells in us. The Holy Spirit is given to lead us to the personal application of the general promises of the Word to our particular personal needs.

Many do not understand this union of the teaching of the Word and the guidance of the Spirit, so that there is a twofold difficulty in knowing what God's will may be. Some seek the will of God by an inner feeling or conviction and want the Spirit to lead them without the Word. Others seek His will in the Word without the living leading of the Holy Spirit. The two must be united—the Word and the Spirit— so that we can know the will of God and learn to pray according to it.

The Word and the Spirit must be joined in our hearts. Only by their indwelling can we experience their teaching. The Word must abide in us. Our life must day by day be under its influence. Not from without but from within comes the quickening of the Word by the Spirit. Only he who yields himself entirely to the supremacy of the Word and the will of God can expect to discern what that will is and to boldly ask in prayer. He who through the Word and the Spirit lives in the will of God by doing it, will know to pray according to that will in the confidence that He hears us.

I long that Christians might see what incalculable harm they do themselves by the thought that because they think their prayer is not according to God's will, they must be content without an answer. God's Word tells us that the great reason for unanswered prayer is that we do not pray in the right way. "When you ask, you do not receive, because you ask with wrong motives" (James 4:3). In not granting an answer, the Father tells us that there is something wrong in our praying. He wants to teach us to find out what is wrong and confess the problem so that He can educate us to believing and prevailing prayer. He can attain His object only when He brings us to see that we are to blame for the withholding of the answer. Our motives or our faith or our life are not what they should be. But this purpose of God is frustrated as long as we are content to say, "Perhaps because my prayer is not according to His will, He does not hear me."

Let us no longer cast the blame of our unanswered prayers on some hidden will of God but rather on our having prayed in error. Allow His Word "When you ask, you do not receive, because you ask with wrong motives" to search your heart and life. Believe that you *can know* if your prayer is according to God's will. Live day by day with the anointing of the Spirit that teaches all things. Then you will understand how the Father's love longs to have His child know His will and to grant the petitions he has asked of Him. "This is the confidence we have in approaching God: that if we ask anything according to his will, he hears us" (1 John 5:14).

There is often great confusion about the will of God.

People think what God wills must inevitably take place. This is by no means the case. A great deal of the blessing that God wills for His people never comes to them. He wills it earnestly, but they do not will it, and so it cannot reach them. This is the great mystery of man being created with a free will. God's will in redemption is also dependent on the will of man. Of God's will revealed in His promises, as much is fulfilled as our faith allows. Prayer is the power that brings to pass that which otherwise would not take place. Faith is the power by which it is decided how much of God's will is effected in us. When once God reveals what He desires to do for us, the responsibility for its execution rests with us.

Some fear this puts too much power into the hands of man. But all power is put into the hands of man in Christ Jesus. The key to all prayer and all power is His. When we come to understand that He is just as much one with us as with the Father, and that we are just as much one with Him as He is with the Father, we will also see how natural and right and safe it is that we are entrusted with so much power in prayer. It is Christ who has the right to ask what He will: it is through our abiding in Him and His abiding in us (in a divine reality of which we have too little understanding) that His Spirit breathes in us what He wants to ask and obtain through us. We pray in His name: the prayers are ours but just as truly His.

Others fear that to believe prayer has such power is to limit the liberty and love of God. If we only knew how we are limiting His liberty and His love by *not* allowing Him to act in the only way in which He chooses to act. I have been asked whether there was not a danger of our thinking that our love for souls and our willingness to see them blessed actually moved God's love and God's willingness to bless them. A good illustration of this happening is the way water runs through water pipes, following the contour and direction of the pipes. The pipes do not make the water willing to flow downward from the hills, nor do they give it its power of refreshment. The pipes determine the water's direction simply by their form and nature. And so it is the very nature of God to love and to bless. His love longs to flow to those in need, but He is dependent upon our prayers to be the conduits of this blessing. He has left it to prayer to specify where the blessing is to flow. He has committed it to His believing people to bring the living water to the desert places. The will of God to bless is dependent upon the will of man to say where the blessing must descend. Such an honor have all his saints. "This is *the confidence* we have in approaching God: that if we ask anything according to his will, he hears us. And if we know that he hears us—whatever we ask—we know that we have what we asked of him" (1 John 5:14–15).

Blessed Master, with my whole heart I thank you for this wonderful lesson: the path to a life full of answers to prayer is through knowing and doing the will of God. Teach me to know your will by living it, loving it, and doing it. Then may I be bold to pray according to your will and find confidence in your answer.

Father, I know it is your will that your children enjoy your presence and blessing. It is your will that everything in the life of your child flow in accordance with your will as the Holy Spirit works this in him. It is your will that your child should live in the daily experience of answers to prayer, so as to enjoy direct fellowship with you. It is your will that your name should be glorified in and through your children. Father, may your will be my confidence in all I ask.

Blessed Savior, teach me to believe in the reality of your will. That your eternal love works out its purpose in each life that yields itself to you. Show me the power behind every promise and every command of the Word and that its fulfillment is sure because God himself guarantees it. Let the will of God be the rock on which my prayer and my assurance of an answer rest. Amen.

Chapter 30

The Ministry of Intercession

You also, like living stones, are being built into a spiritual
house to be a holy priesthood, offering spiritual sacrifices
acceptable to God through Jesus Christ.

1 Peter 2:5

You will be called priests of the Lord.

Isaiah 61:6

The Spirit of the Lord is on me, because he has anointed me.

Luke 4:18

The words in Luke are Jesus' words. As the fruit of His work all redeemed ones are priests, fellow-partakers with Him of His anointing with the Spirit as High Priest. "It is like precious oil running down on Aaron's beard, down upon the collar of his robes" (Psalm 133:2). As did every son of Aaron, so does every member of Jesus' body have a right to the priesthood. But not everyone exercises it. Many are still entirely ignorant of it. And yet it is the highest privilege and likeness to Him who "lives to intercede" (Hebrews 7:25). Do you doubt this is true? Think what constitutes the priesthood.

First, there is the *work of the priesthood*. This has two sides: Godward and manward. "Every high priest . . . is *appointed for men* in things *pertaining to God*" (Hebrews 5:1 NKJV); or as it is said by Moses: "The Lord set apart the tribe of Levi . . . *to stand before the Lord* to minister and to *pronounce blessings in his name*" (Deuteronomy 10:8; see also 21:5; 33:10; Malachi 2:6–7). On the one hand the priest had the power to draw near to God, to dwell with Him in His house, and to present before Him the blood of the sacrifice or the burning incense. He did not do this work on his own behalf, but for the sake of the people whose representative he was. This is the other side of his work. He received from the people their sacrifices, presented them before God, and then came out to bless in His name, to give the assurance of His favor and to teach them His law.

So a priest is a man who does not live for himself. *He lives with God and for God.* His work is as God's servant to care for His house, His honor, and His worship, and to make known to men His love and His will. *He identifies with others and serves them* (Hebrews 5:2). His work is to discover what sins trouble people so that he can bring them before God and offer sacrifices and incense in their name in order to obtain forgiveness and blessing for them, and then to bless them in His name. This is the high calling of every believer. "This is the glory of all his saints" (Psalm 149:9). They are redeemed for the purpose of being God's priests in the midst of the perishing around them. In conformity to Jesus, the

Great High Priest, God's priests are to be the ministers and stewards of His grace.

There is also *the walk of the priesthood* in harmony with its work. As God is holy, so the priest is to be holy. This means not only separated from everything unclean but also *holy unto God*, being set apart and given up to God for His use. The separation from the world and setting apart unto God was indicated in many ways.

First, it was seen in their clothing: the rich garments, made of fine linen, were made after God's own design, and these marked them as His own (Exodus 28). Second, it was seen in the requirements for their special purity and freedom from all contact with death and defilement (Leviticus 21). Much that was allowed to an ordinary Israelite was forbidden to the priests. Third, was the injunction that a priest must have no physical defect or blemish; this perfection was to be a type of wholeness and holiness in God's service. Fourth, was the arrangement by which the priestly tribes were to have no inheritance with other tribes; God alone was to be their inheritance. Their life was lived by faith; set apart unto God, they were to live in Him and for Him.

All of this composed a sign of what the character of the New Testament priest is to be. Our priestly power with God depends on our personal life and walk. We must be those of whose walk on earth Jesus says, "You have a few people . . . who have not soiled their clothes" (Revelation 3:4).

In the surrender of what may appear lawful to others in our separation from the world, we prove that our consecration of holiness to the Lord is wholehearted and complete. The physical perfection of the priest has its counterpart in our being "without defect"; "without stain or wrinkle or any other blemish, but holy and blameless"; "the man of God may be thoroughly equipped for every good work"; "mature and complete, not lacking anything" (Leviticus 21:17–21; Ephesians 5:27; 2 Timothy 3:17; James 1:4). Above all, we consent to give up all inheritance on earth, to forsake all, and like Christ, to have only God as our portion. To possess as not possessing and hold all for God alone marks the true priest, the man who only lives for God and his fellowmen.

In Aaron God had chosen all his sons to be priests. Each of them was a priest by birth, but he could not enter into his work without a special act of consecration. Every child of God is a priest by right of his birth, by his blood relationship to the Great High Priest. But this is not enough—he will exercise his power only as he accepts and realizes his consecration.

With Aaron and his sons it took place this way (Exodus 29): After being washed and clothed, they were anointed with the holy oil. Sacrifices were offered. Then the right ear, the right hand, and the right foot were anointed with the blood. Again, the garments were sprinkled with the blood and the oil together. As the child of God understands more fully what the blood and the Spirit, of which he is already a partaker, are to him, the power of the Holy Priesthood will work in him. The blood takes away all sense of unworthiness; the Spirit, all sense of inadequacy.

Let us note what was new about the application of the blood to the priest. When before he came as a penitent sinner, bringing a sacrifice for his sin and seeking forgiveness, the blood was sprinkled on the altar but not on his person. Now, for priestly consecration, there was to be closer contact with the blood. Ear, hand, and foot were by a special act brought under its power, and the whole being taken possession of and sanctified for God. So when the believer, who had been content to think chiefly of the blood sprinkled on the mercy seat as enough for his pardon, is led to seek full priestly access to God, he feels the need of a fuller and more abiding experience of the power of the blood. He needs a true sprinkling and cleansing of the heart from an evil conscience so that he no longer feels any guilt for his sins. As he begins to enjoy this, his consciousness is awakened to his wonderful right of intimate access to God and the full assurance that his intercession is acceptable.

As the blood gives the right, the Spirit gives the power and equips us for believing prayer. He breathes into us the priestly spirit: burning love for God's honor and the saving of souls. He makes us so one with Jesus that prayer in His name is a reality. He strengthens us for believing, persistent prayer. The more the Christian is truly filled with the Spirit of Christ, the more spontaneous will be his life of priestly intercession. Beloved fellow Christians, God needs priests who will draw near to Him, who will live in His presence, and by their intercession bring down the blessing of His grace on a waiting world. The world needs priests who will bear the burden of the perishing and intercede mightily on their behalf.

Are you willing to offer yourself for this work? You know the surrender it demands: nothing less than the Christlike giving up of all, so that the saving purposes of God's love may be accomplished among all peoples. Do not be any longer one of those who are content with their own salvation and who work just enough to keep themselves warm and alive. Let nothing keep you back from giving yourselves to be wholly and only priests of the Most High God. The thought of unworthiness, of inadequacy, need not keep you back. Through the blood, the objective power of the perfect redemption works in you. Through the Spirit, its full subjective personal experience of a divine life is demonstrated. The blood provides an infinite worthiness to make your prayers most acceptable. The Spirit provides a divine fitness, teaching you to pray according to the will of God. *Every priest knew that when he presented a sacrifice according to the law of the sanctuary, it was accepted.* Under the covering of the blood of Christ and His Spirit, you have the assurance that all the wonderful promises concerning prayer in the name of Jesus will be fulfilled in you. Abiding in union with the Great High Priest, "You may ask . . . for anything in [His] name, and [He] will do it" (John 14:13). You will have power to pray the effectual prayer of the righteous man that avails much. You will not only join in the general prayer of the church for the world but also be able in your own area of influence take up your special work of prayer—as priests, to make transactions with God, to receive and know the answers, and so to bless others in His name. Come and be a priest for God. Seek to walk before Him in the full consciousness that you have been set apart for the ministry of intercession. This is the true blessedness of conformity to the image of God's Son.

My blessed High Priest, accept the consecration in which my soul now would respond to your message.

I believe in the holy priesthood of your saints. I believe that I too am a priest with power to appear before the Father, and in the prayer that avails much to bring down blessing on the perishing around me.

I believe in the power of your precious blood to cleanse me from all sin, to give me perfect confidence toward God, and bring me close in the full assurance of faith that my intercession will be heard.

I believe in the anointing of the Spirit, coming down daily from you, my Great High Priest, to sanctify me, to fill me with the consciousness of my priestly calling, and with love for souls, to teach me what is according to God's will, and how to pray the prayer of faith.

I believe that as you, Lord Jesus, are in all things my life, so you are also the surety for my prayer life. You will include me in the fellowship of your wondrous work of intercession.

In this faith, I yield myself this day to my God as one of His anointed priests, to stand before His face and to intercede on behalf of sinners and to bless them in His name.

Holy Lord Jesus, accept and seal my consecration. Lay your hands upon me and consecrate me to this holy work. Let me walk among men with the consciousness and the character of a priest of the Most High God.

"To him who loves us and has freed us from our sins by his blood, and has made us to be a kingdom and priests to serve his God and Father—to him be glory and power for ever and ever! Amen."

Chapter 31

A Life of Prayer

Be joyful always; pray continually; give thanks
in all circumstances.

1 Thessalonians 5:16–18

Our Lord gave the parable of the widow and the unjust judge to teach us that we should always pray and not give up (Luke 18:1–5). As the widow persevered in seeking one particular thing, the parable seems to refer to persevering prayer for a particular blessing when God seems to delay or appears to refuse. The words in the Epistles, which speak of continuing instant in prayer, continuing in prayer and watching in the same, of praying always in the Spirit, appear to refer more to the whole life being one of prayer. As the soul fills with longing for the manifestation of God's glory to us and in us, through us and around us, and with the confidence that He hears the prayers of His children, the inner life of the soul is continually rising upward in dependence and faith, in longing desire and trustful expectation.

What is needed to live such a life of prayer? The first thing is undoubtedly the entire sacrifice of one's life to God's kingdom and glory. He who seeks to pray without ceasing simply because he wants to be very pious and good, will never attain to it. It is by forgetting oneself and yielding one's life to live for God and His honor that the heart is enlarged to know the light of God and His will. It is the recognition that everything around us needs God's help and blessing; that all adversity is an opportunity for His being glorified. Because everything is weighed and tested by the one thing that fills the heart—the glory of God—and because the soul has learned that only what is of God can honor Him, the whole life becomes one of looking up, of crying from the inmost heart for God to prove His power and love and show forth His glory. The believer awakens to the consciousness that he is one of the watchmen on Zion's walls, one of the Lord's remembrancers, whose call really does touch and move the King in heaven to do what would otherwise not be done. He understands how real Paul's exhortation was: "Pray in the Spirit on all occasions with all kinds of prayers and requests. With this in mind, be alert and always keep on praying for all the saints" (Ephesians 6:18), and "Devote yourselves to prayer . . . and pray for us, too" (Colossians 4:2–3). To forget oneself, to live for God and His kingdom among men, is the way to learn to pray without ceasing.

This life devoted to God must be accompanied by the deep confidence that our prayer is effective. In His prayer lessons, our Lord insisted upon nothing so much as faith in God as a Father who most certainly does what we ask. "Ask and you will receive" (John 16:24); to count confidently on an answer is with Him the beginning and the end of His teaching (compare Matthew 7:8 and John 16:24). In proportion as this assurance masters us, and it becomes a settled thing that our prayers count, and that God does what we ask, we dare not neglect the use of this wonderful power. The soul turns wholly to God, and our life becomes a prayer. We see that the Lord takes time because we, and all around us, are creatures of time, under the law of growth. Knowing that not one prayer of faith will be lost, that there is sometimes a need for the storing up and accumulating of prayer, but recognizing that persevering prayer is irresistible, prayer becomes the quiet, persistent living of our life of desire and faith in the presence of our God.

Let us no longer by our human reasoning limit and weaken such free and sure promises of the living God, robbing them of their power and ourselves of the wonderful confidence they are meant to inspire. Not in God, not in His secret will, not in the limitations of His promises, but in *us* is the hindrance. We are not what we should be to obtain the promise. Let us open our whole heart to God's words of promise in all their simplicity and truth. They will search us and humble us. They will lift us up and make us glad and strong. To the faith that knows it gets what it asks, prayer is not work or a burden but a joy and a triumph. It becomes second nature.

This union of strong desire and firm confidence is nothing but the life of the Holy Spirit within us. The Spirit dwells in us, hides himself in the depths of our being, and stirs our desire after the unseen and the divine, after God himself. Whether in groanings that cannot be uttered, or in clear and conscious assurance; whether in special petitions for the deeper revelation of Christ to us, or in pleadings for a soul, a work, the church, or the world, prayer is always and only the work of the Holy Spirit. He draws out the heart to thirst for God, to long for His being made known and glorified.

Where the child of God truly lives and walks in the Spirit, where he is not content to remain carnal, but seeks to be spiritual, in everything a fit organ for the divine Spirit to reveal the life of Christ and Christ himself, there the never-ceasing intercession life of the blessed Son is revealed and then repeats itself in our experience. Because it is the Spirit of Christ who prays in us, our prayer must be heard; because it is we who pray in the Spirit, there is need of time, and patience, and continual renewing of the prayer until every obstacle is conquered and the harmony between God's Spirit and ours is perfect.

But the most important thing we need for such a life of unceasing prayer is to know that Jesus teaches us to pray. We have begun to understand a little of what *His* teaching is. It is not the communication of new thoughts or views, not the discovery of failure or error, not the stirring up of desire and faith—however important all of this is—but by receiving us into the fellowship of His own prayer life before the Father, Jesus teaches to pray.

It was the sight of Jesus praying that stirred up their desire, that made the disciples long for and ask to be taught how to pray. It is the faith of the ever-praying Jesus, to whom belongs the power to pray, that teaches us to pray. It is because He who prays is our Head and our Life. All He has is ours and is given to us when we give ourselves to Him. By His blood He leads us into the immediate presence of God. The inner sanctuary is our home; we dwell there. He that lives so near to God, and knows that He has been brought near to bless those who are far away, cannot help but pray. Christ makes us partakers with himself of His prayer power and prayer life. We understand then that our true aim must not be to work more, or to pray enough to keep the work on track, but to pray more and then work enough for the power and blessing obtained in prayer to find its way through us to others. It is Christ who ever lives to pray, who saves and reigns. He communicates His prayer life to us. He maintains it in us if we trust Him. He is the strength of our praying without ceasing. Christ teaches us to pray by showing how He does it, by doing it in us, by leading us to do it through Him and as He does. Christ is the life and the strength of a never-ceasing prayer life.

The sight of our ever-praying Lord as our life enables us to pray without ceasing. Because His priesthood is the power of an endless life, that resurrection life that never fades and never fails, and because His life is our life, praying without ceasing can become to us nothing less than the joy of heaven. So the apostle says, "Be joyful *always*; pray *continually*; give thanks *in all circumstances*" (1 Thessalonians 5:16–18). Borne up between the never-ceasing joy and the never-ceasing praise, never-ceasing prayer is the manifestation of the power of eternal life. The union between the Vine and the branch is a prayer union. The highest conformity to Christ, the most blessed participation in the glory of His heavenly life is that we take part in His work of intercession. In the experience of our union with Him, praying without ceasing becomes not only a possibility but also a reality, the holiest and most blessed part of our fellowship with God. We make our abode within the veil in the presence of the Father. What the Father says, we do; what the Son says, the Father does. Praying without ceasing is the earthly manifestation of heaven come down, the foretaste of the life where they do not rest day or night in the song of worship and adoration.

Father, with my whole heart I praise you for this wondrous life of never-ceasing prayer, never-ceasing fellowship, never-ceasing answers, and never-ceasing experience of my oneness with Him who ever lives to pray. God, help me to dwell and walk in the presence of your glory always so that prayer may be the spontaneous expression of my life with you.

Blessed Savior, with my whole heart I praise you that you came from heaven to share with me in my needs and the cries of my heart, that I might share with you in your all-prevailing intercession. And I thank you that you have taken me into the school of prayer to teach the blessedness and the power of a life that is prayer. Thank you for taking me up into the fellowship of your life of intercession, so that through me your blessings may be dispensed to those around me.

Holy Spirit, with deep reverence I thank you for your work in me. Through you I am allowed to share in the intimate relationship between the Son and the Father, and enter into the fellowship of the life and love of the Trinity. Spirit of God, perfect your work in me; bring me into perfect union with Christ my Intercessor. Let your constant indwelling make my life one of constant intercession so that I may glorify you on earth and bless others with the blessing you have given me. Amen.

Appendix:
George Müller and the Secret of His Power in Prayer

When God wishes to remind His church of a truth that is not being understood or practiced, He usually does so by using someone to be in word and deed a living witness to that truth. So God raised up in the nineteenth century, among others, George Müller to demonstrate that God is indeed the One who hears our prayers. I know of no way in which the principal truths of God's Word in regard to prayer can be more effectively illustrated and established than a short review of Müller's life and his prayer experiences.

Müller was born in Prussia on September 25, 1805, and died on March 10, 1898, at the age of ninety-two. His early life, even after having entered the University of Halle as a theological student, was wicked in the extreme. When just twenty years old, a friend took him to a prayer meeting. He was deeply impressed, and soon after that came to know the Savior. Soon he began reading missionary newsletters and articles, and in due course offered himself to the London Society for promoting Christianity to the Jews. He was accepted as a student, but soon found that he could not submit to the rules of the Society in all things because he felt they left too little liberty for the leading of the Holy Spirit. The connection was dissolved in 1830 by mutual consent, and he became the pastor of a small congregation at Teignmouth. In 1832 he was led to Bristol. There as pastor of Bethesda Chapel, he was led to work in their orphan home, in which connection God so remarkably led him to trust His Word and to experience answers to prayer.

A few adapted quotations in regard to his spiritual life will prepare us to receive the testimony of his experiences in reference to prayer:

"In connection with this, I would mention that the Lord very graciously gave me, from the very commencement of my spiritual life, a measure of simplicity and of childlike disposition in spiritual things, so that while I was exceedingly ignorant of the Scriptures, and was still from time to time overcome by some outward sins, I was able to carry most matters to the Lord in prayer. I have found godliness profitable for all things, having promise for our present life and for the one that is to come. Though very weak and ignorant, I had by now, by the grace of God, some desire to bring benefit to others, and I who so faithfully once served Satan, sought now to win souls for Christ."

At Teignmouth he was led to know how to use God's Word and to trust the Holy Spirit as the teacher given by God to make the Word clear. He writes,

"God then began to show me that the Word of God alone is our standard of judgment in spiritual things; that it can be explained only by the Holy Spirit, and that in our day, as well as in former times, He is the teacher of His people. I had not experimentally understood the office of the Holy Spirit before that time.

"But when I understood, it had a great effect on me, for the Lord enabled me to put it to the test by laying aside commentaries and almost every other book, and simply reading the Word of God and studying it.

"The result was that the first evening I shut myself in my room to give myself to prayer and meditation of the Scriptures. I learned more in a few hours than I had previously learned over a period of several months. But the particular difference was that I received real strength for my soul in so doing. I now began to try or test, as it were, the principles and teachings I had learned and seen in the Scriptures and found that they stood the test."

He writes of obedience to the Word of God in connection with his being baptized:

"It had pleased God in His abundant mercy to bring me into a state of willingness to carry out in my life whatever I found in the Scriptures. I could say, 'I will do His will,' and it was on that basis, I believe, that I saw what doctrines were of God. I want to point out here that the passage that was such a help to me along this line was John 7:17. It has been a most remarkable comment to me on many doctrines and precepts of our faith. For instance, 'Do not resist an evil person. If someone strikes you on the right cheek, turn to him the other also. And if someone wants to sue you and take your tunic, let him have your cloak as well. If someone forces you to go one mile, go with him two miles. Give to the one who asks you, and do not turn away from the one who wants to borrow from you. You have heard that it was said, "Love your neighbor and hate your enemy." But I tell you: Love your enemies and pray for those who persecute you'

(Matthew 5:39–44). 'Sell your possessions and give to the poor' (Luke 12:33). 'Let no debt remain outstanding, except the continuing debt to love one another' (Romans 13:8). The state of mind enjoined in John 7:17 will cause any objections to vanish. Whoever is willing to act out these commandments of the Lord *literally*, will, I believe, be led with me to see that to take them literally is the will of God. Those who do take them in this way will doubtless enter into difficulties that are hard on the flesh, but these difficulties will have the tendency to remind them that they are strangers and pilgrims here, that this world is not their home, and so to throw themselves more upon God, who will surely help us through any difficulty into which we may be brought by seeking to act in obedience to His Word."

This implicit surrender to God's Word led Müller to certain views and conduct with regard to money that profoundly influenced his future life. They had their root in the conviction that money was a divine stewardship, and that all money had therefore to be received and dispensed in direct fellowship with God himself. This led him to the adoption of the following four rules:

1. *Do not receive any fixed salary*, both because in the collecting of it there is often much that is at variance with the free-will offering with which God's service is to be maintained and in the receiving of it a danger of placing more dependence on human sources of income than on the living God.

2. *Never ask any human being for help*, however great the need might be, but make your wants and needs known to God alone, who has promised to care for His servants and to hear their prayers.

3. *Take literally the command of Luke 12:33: "Sell your pos-*

sessions and give to the poor," and never save up money, but spend all God has entrusted to you on the poor and on the work of His kingdom.

4. *Take literally Romans 13:8, "Let no debt remain outstanding,"* and never buy on credit or be in debt for anything, but trust God alone to provide.

This style of living was not easy at first, but Müller testifies that it was instrumental in bringing his soul to rest in God and to draw it into closer union with Him when he was inclined to backslide.

He found it was impossible to live in sin and at the same time live in such communion with God so as to draw everything he needed for his livelihood.

Not long after his settlement at Bristol, the Scriptural Knowledge Institution for Home and Abroad was established for aiding in day school, Sunday school, missions, and Bible work. The orphan work for which Müller became best known was a branch of this institution. In 1834 his heart was touched by the case of an orphan brought to Christ in one of the schools but who had to go to a poorhouse, where his spiritual needs would not be cared for. Shortly afterward he wrote, on November 20, 1835, "Today it has been laid on my heart to no longer merely *think* about the establishment of an orphan home, but actually to set about seeing to it, and I have been much in prayer with respect to it in order to ascertain the Lord's mind. May God make it plain." And on November 25, "I have been again much in prayer, yesterday and today, about the orphan home, and am more and more convinced that it is of God. May He in mercy guide me. The three chief reasons are: (1) That God may be glorified, should He be pleased to furnish me with the means, seeing that it is not a vain thing to trust Him; and that in this way the faith of His children may be strengthened. (2) That the spiritual welfare of fatherless and motherless children may be met. (3) That the temporal welfare of these children may also be attended to."

After some months of prayer and waiting on God, a house was rented with room for thirty children, and in course of time three more, with room for 120 children. The work was carried on in this way for ten years, the supplies for the needs of the orphans being asked and received of God alone. It was often a time of pressing need and much prayer, but a trial of faith more precious than of gold was found unto the praise and honor and glory of God. The Lord was preparing His servant for greater things. By God's providence and His Holy Spirit, Müller was led to desire, and to wait upon God until he received from Him, the sure promise of £15,000 for the purchase of a home to house 300 children. This first home was opened in 1849. In 1858, a second and a third home, for 950 more orphans, was opened, costing £35,000. And in 1869 and 1870, a fourth and a fifth home, for 850 more children, at an expense of £58,000, bringing the total number of orphans to 2,100.

In addition to this work, God gave Müller almost as much money for other works, such as the support of schools and missions and for Bible tract circulation. In all, he received from God to be spent in His work more than one million pounds sterling. How little he knew that when he gave up his little salary of £30 a year in obedience to the leading of God's Word and His Holy Spirit, what God was preparing to give him as the reward of his obedience and faith, and how wonderfully the Word was to be fulfilled to him: " 'Well done, my good servant!' his master replied. 'Because you have been trustworthy in a very small matter, take charge of ten cities'" (Luke 19:17).

And these things have happened for an example to us. God calls us to be followers of men like George Müller, even as he was of Christ. His God is our God; the same promises are for us; the same service of love and faith in which he labored may be His calling for us. Let us look at the way in which God gave George Müller such power as a man of prayer. We will find in it some remarkable illustrations of the very lessons we have been studying in this book. We will especially have impressed upon us His first great lesson, that if we will come to Him in the way He has pointed out, with definite petitions, made known to us by the Spirit through the Word as being according to the will of God, we may confidently believe that whatever we ask will be done.

Prayer and the Word of God

We have repeatedly seen that God's listening to our voice depends upon our listening to His voice. (See chapters 22 and 23.) We must not only have a special promise to plead when we make a special request, but our whole life must be under the supremacy of the Word. The testimony of George Müller on this point is very instructive. He tells us how the discovery of the true place of the Word of God and the teaching of the Spirit with it was the commencement of a new era in his spiritual life. Of it he writes,

"Now the scriptural way of reasoning would have been: God himself has condescended to become an author, and I am ignorant about that precious Book that His Holy Spirit has caused to be written through the instrumentality of His servants. It contains what I ought to know, the knowledge of which will lead me to true happiness; therefore, I ought to read it again and again most earnestly, most prayerfully, and with meditation; and in this practice I ought to continue all the days of my life. For I was aware that though I read it some, I knew scarcely anything of it. But instead of acting thus and being led by my ignorance of the Word of God to study it more, my difficulty in understanding it and the little enjoyment I had in it made me careless of reading it (for much prayerful reading of the Word gives not merely more knowledge but increases the delight we have in reading it); and so like many believers, I practically preferred for the first four years of my spiritual life the works of uninspired men to the oracles of the living God. The consequence was that I remained a babe both in knowledge and in grace. In knowledge, I say, for all *true* knowledge comes by the Spirit through the Word. And because I neglected the Word, I was for nearly four years so ignorant that I did not *clearly* know even the *fundamental* points of our faith. This lack of knowledge sadly kept me back from walking steadily in the ways of God. For when it pleased the Lord in August 1829 to bring me truly to the Scriptures, my life and walk became very different. And though ever since that time I have fallen short of what I might and ought to be, yet by the grace of God I have been enabled to live much closer to Him than before. If any believer is reading this who prefers other books to the Holy Scriptures, and who enjoys the writings of men more than the Word of God, may they be forewarned by my loss. I will consider this book to have been the means of doing good, if it please the Lord through its instrumentality to lead some of His people to no longer neglect the Holy Scriptures but to give them that preference that they have until now given to the writings of mere mortals.

"Before I leave this subject, I would only add, if the reader understands very little of the Word of God, he ought to read it more; for the Spirit explains the Word by the Word. And if he enjoys the reading of the Word little, that is good reason to read it more; for the frequent reading of the Scriptures creates a delight in them so that the more we read them, the more we desire to do so.

"Above all, he should seek to have it settled in his own mind that God alone by His Spirit can teach him, and that as God will be inquired of for blessings, it becomes him to seek God's blessing before reading and also while reading.

"He should also realize that although the Holy Spirit is the best and most sufficient teacher, He does not always teach something when *we* desire it, and so we may have to ask Him again and again for the explanation of certain passages; but He will surely teach us if we are seeking for light prayerfully, patiently, and with a view to the glory of God."*

We find in Müller's journal frequent mention made of two and three hours spent in prayer over the Word for the nurturing of his spiritual life. As the fruit of this, when he needed strength and encouragement in prayer, the individual promises were not to him mere arguments from a book to be used with God. They were living words that he had heard the Father's living voice speak to him, and which he could now bring to the Father in living faith.

Prayer and the Will of God

One of the greatest difficulties of young believers is to know whether what they desire is according to God's will. One of the most precious lessons God wants to teach through the experience of George Müller is that He is willing

---

*These extracts are adapted from a work in four volumes: *The Lord's Dealings With George Müller* (London: Nisbet & Co.). No further publication information is available.

to make known things of which His Word says nothing directly, that they are His will for us, and that we may ask for them. The teaching of the Spirit (not without or against the Word) is above, beyond, and in addition to it, without which we cannot know God's will. It is the heritage of every believer. It is through *the Word, and the Word alone*, that the Spirit teaches, applying the general principles or promises to our special need. And it is *the Spirit, and the Spirit alone*, who can truly make the Word a light to our path, whether it is the path of duty in our daily walk or the path of faith in our approach to God. Let us notice in what childlike simplicity and teachableness the discovery of God's will was so clearly made known to Müller.

With regard to the building of the first home and the assurance he had of its being God's will, he wrote in May 1850, just after it had been opened. Speaking of the great difficulties there were and how unlikely it appeared that they would be naturally removed, he said, "But while the prospect before me would have been overwhelming had I looked at it naturally, I was never once permitted to question how it would end. For as from the beginning I was sure *it was the will of God* that I should proceed with the work of building this large orphan home, so also from the beginning I was certain that it would be finished as if the home had already been filled."

The way he found out what God's will was comes out with special clarity in his account of the building of the second home:

"*December 5, 1850.* Under these circumstances I can only pray that the Lord in His tender mercy would not allow Satan to gain an advantage over me. By the grace of God my heart says, *Lord, if I could be sure that it is your will that I should go forward in this matter, I would do so cheerfully; and, on the other hand, if I could be sure that these are vain, foolish, proud thoughts, that they are not from you, I would by your grace hate them and entirely put them aside.*

"My hope is in God: He will help and teach me. Judging, however, from His former dealings with me, it would not be a strange thing to me, nor surprising, if He called me to work toward an even larger project.

"Thoughts about enlarging the orphan work have not yet come up even though an abundance of money has lately come in; for over about seven weeks I waited upon God while comparatively very little came in, and about four times as much was going out in expenses. Had the Lord not previously sent large sums, we would have been very distressed indeed.

"Lord, how can your servant know your will in this matter? Will you be pleased to teach him?

"*December 11.* During the last six days I have been day after day waiting upon God concerning this matter. It has generally been more or less all day on my heart. When I have been awake at night, it has not been far from my thoughts. And yet all of this has been without the least bit of anxiety. I am perfectly calm and quiet about it. My soul would be happy to go forward in this service if I could be sure that the Lord would have me do so; for then, notwithstanding the numerous difficulties, all would be well, and His name would be magnified.

"On the other hand, were I assured that the Lord would have me to be satisfied with my present sphere of service, and that I should not pray about enlarging the work, by His grace I would not pray about expanding it; by His grace I could, without any effort, cheerfully yield to it; for He has brought me into such a state of heart that I only desire to please Him in this matter. Moreover, until now I have not spoken about this thing even to my beloved wife, the sharer of my joys, sorrows, and labors for more than twenty years; nor is it likely that I will do so for some time to come. For I prefer quietly to wait on the Lord without conversing on the subject in order that I may be kept the more easily by His blessing from being influenced by things from without. The burden of my prayer concerning this matter is that the Lord would not allow me to make a mistake, and that He would teach me to do His will.

"*December 26.* Fifteen days have elapsed since I wrote the preceding paragraph. Every day since then I have continued to pray about this matter with a good measure of earnestness, by the help of God. I have the fullest and most peaceful assurance that He will clearly show me His will. This evening I have had again an especially solemn season of prayer to seek to know the will of God. But while I continue to entreat and beseech the Lord that He would not allow me to be deluded in this business, I may say I have scarcely any doubt remaining in my mind as to what will be the outcome, even that I should go forward in this matter. As this, however, is one of the most momentous steps that I have ever taken, I perceive that I cannot go about it with too much caution, prayerfulness, and deliberation. I am in no hurry about it. I could wait for years, by God's grace, were this His will, before even taking one step toward this thing, or even speaking to anyone about it; and on the other hand, I would set to work tomorrow were the Lord to tell me to do so. This calmness of mind, this having no will of my own in the matter, this only wishing to please my heavenly Father in it, this only seeking His and not my honor in it; this state of heart,

I say, is the fullest assurance that I am not under the influence of the flesh, but that if I am helped to go on, *I will know the will of God completely.* But while I write this, I cannot but add at the same time that I do crave the honor and the glorious privilege to be more and more used by the Lord.

"I desire to be allowed to provide scriptural instruction for a thousand orphans instead of only 300. I desire to expound the Holy Scriptures regularly to a thousand orphans, instead of 300. I desire that it may be even more abundantly clear that God is still the hearer and answerer of prayer, and that He is the living God now as He ever was and ever will be, when He shall simply, in answer to prayer, have condescended to provide me with a house for 700 orphans and with the means to support them. This last consideration is the most important point in my mind. The Lord's honor is the principal point with me in this whole matter; and because this is the case, if He would be more glorified by my not going forward in this business, I would by His grace be perfectly content to give up all thoughts about it. *Surely in such a state of mind, obtained by the Holy Spirit, you will, my heavenly Father, not suffer your child to be mistaken, much less deluded.* By the help of God I will continue day by day to further wait upon Him in prayer concerning this thing, until He tells me to act.

"*January 2, 1851.* During this week I have been helped day by day, and more than once every day, to seek the guidance of the Lord about another orphan house. The burden of my prayer has still been that He in His great mercy would keep me from making a mistake. During the last week the book of Proverbs has come in the course of my Scripture reading, and my heart has been refreshed in reference to this subject by the following passage: 'Trust in the Lord with all your heart and lean not on your own understanding; in all your ways acknowledge him, and he will make your paths straight' (Proverbs 3:5–6). By the grace of God I do acknowledge the Lord in all my ways, and in this issue in particular. I have, therefore, the comfortable assurance that He will direct my paths concerning this part of my service, as to whether I shall be occupied in it or not. Further, 'the integrity of the upright guides them' (Proverbs 11:3). By the grace of God I am upright in this business. My honest purpose is to get glory for God. Therefore, I expect to be guided aright. Further, 'commit to the Lord whatever you do, and your plans will succeed' (Proverbs 16:3). I do commit what I do to the Lord. My heart is more and more coming to a calm, quiet, and settled assurance that the Lord will condescend to use me still further in the orphan work. Here, Lord, is your servant."

When later he decided to build two additional houses, he wrote as follows:

"I have still kept this matter entirely to myself. Though it is now about seven weeks since my mind has been occupied with it, and since I have been daily praying about it, yet not one other human being knows of it. This evening has been particularly set apart for prayer, beseeching the Lord once more not to allow me to be mistaken in this endeavor, and much less to be deluded by the devil. I have also sought to let all the reasons *against* building another orphan house and all the reasons *for* doing so pass before my mind. For clarity, I will write them down. . . .

"As much as the nine previous reasons are valid to me, they could not decide it for me were there not one more: I am at peace. After having for months pondered the matter, and having looked at it from every angle and in light of every difficulty, and then having been finally led, after much prayer, to decide on this enlargement, my mind is at peace. I who have again and again sought my heavenly Father not to allow me to be deluded, or even to make a mistake, am at perfect peace concerning this decision. It is an assurance that has come after much prayer over a period of weeks and months, and I believe is the leading of the Holy Spirit. I purpose to go forward, believing that I will not be disappointed, because I trust in God. Many and great may be the difficulties; thousands of prayers may have ascended to God before the full answer is obtained; much exercise of faith and patience may be required; but in the end it will again be seen, that I, His servant, who trusts in Him, has not been disappointed."

Prayer and the Glory of God

We have tried more than once to emphasize this truth: Ordinarily we seek the reasons for our prayers not being heard in whether or not we have asked according to the will of God. Scripture warns us to find the cause in ourselves— in our not being in the right spiritual state or our not asking with the right motive. The thing may be in full accordance with His will, but the asking or the spirit of the one who asks may not; therefore, we are not heard. Just as the root of all sin is self and self-seeking, so there is nothing in our more spiritual desires that so effectually hinders God's answering as praying for our own pleasure or glory. Prayer, to have power and to prevail, must ask for the glory of God. And one can only pray this way when he is living for the glory of God.

In the life of George Müller we have one of the most remarkable instances on record of God's Holy Spirit leading a man deliberately and systematically to make the glorifying of God his first and only object. Ponder well what he says, and learn the lesson God would teach us through him:

"I constantly had cases brought before me that proved that one of the special needs of the children of God in our day was to have their faith strengthened. I longed, therefore, to have something to point my brethren to as a visible proof that our God and Father is the same faithful God as He ever has been and that He is as willing as ever to prove himself to be the living God to all who put their trust in Him.

"My spirit longed to be instrumental in strengthening their faith by giving them not only instances from the Word of God of His willingness and ability to help all who rely upon Him but also to show them that He is the same in our day. I knew that the Word of God ought to be enough, and it was by grace enough for me; but still I felt that I ought to lend a helping hand to my brethren.

"I therefore judged myself bound to be the servant of the church of Christ in the particular area in which I had obtained mercy; namely, in being able to take God at His Word and rely upon it. The first object of the work was, and still is, that God might be magnified by the fact that the orphans under my care are provided with all they need—*by prayer and faith without anyone being asked*—thereby it may be seen that God is faithful and hears our prayers.

"When I began the orphan work in 1835, my main objective was the glory of God, by giving a practical demonstration as to what could be accomplished simply through the instrumentality of prayer and faith, in order to benefit the church at large and to lead a careless world to see the reality of the things of God by showing them that God is the living God. My aim has been abundantly honored. Thousands of sinners have been converted, and thousands of God's children in all parts of the world have been benefited by this work, even as I had anticipated. But the larger the work has grown, the greater the blessing has been bestowed in the very way in which I looked for it: for the attention of hundreds of thousands has been drawn to the work, and many tens of thousands have come to see it. All of this leads me to desire to continue to labor on in this way in order to bring greater glory to the name of the Lord. That He may be seen, magnified, admired, trusted, and relied on at all times is my aim in this service, and particularly in this projected enlargement of the work. That it may be seen how much one man—simply by trusting in God—can bring about through prayer, and how other children of God may also be led to carry on the work of God in dependence upon Him. That God's children may be led increasingly to trust Him in their individual situations and circumstances—for this reason, I am led to proceed with this amplification of the facility."

Prayer and Trust in God

The final point that I would emphasize from Mr. Müller's narrative is the lesson of firm and unwavering trust in God's promise as the secret of persevering prayer. If once we have in submission to the teaching of the Spirit in the Word taken hold of God's promise and believed that the Father has heard us, we must not allow ourselves through delay or unfavorable appearances to be shaken in our faith.

"The full answer to my daily prayers was far from being realized, yet there was abundant encouragement granted by the Lord to continue in prayer. But suppose far less had come in than did come in for the work? Coming to the conclusion upon scriptural grounds and much prayer and self-examination that what we ask for is according to the will of God, we ought to persevere with faith and patience, believing that we will receive it in due time.

"And so I am now waiting upon God for certain blessings for which I have daily sought Him for ten years and six months without one day's intermission. The full answer is not yet given concerning the conversion of certain individuals, though in the meantime I have received thousands of answers to prayer. I have also prayed daily without ceasing for the conversion of other individuals for six or seven years, for others from two to three years; and still the answer is not yet granted concerning those persons, while in the meantime many prayers have been answered and souls converted for whom I had been praying. I emphasize this fact for the benefit of those who may think that I need only to ask God, and I receive at once; or that I might pray concerning anything, and the answer always comes.

"One can only expect to obtain answers to prayers that are according to the mind of God; and even then, patience and faith may be exercised for many years, even as mine are exercised in the matter to which I have referred; and yet I am daily continuing in prayer and expecting the answer to the point that I have often thanked God for giving it, even though I may have prayed for it for nineteen years. Be encouraged, dear Christians, to give yourselves to prayer with fresh determination; only be sure that you ask things that are for the glory of God.

"The most remarkable answer right now is that the funds from Scotland have supplied me, as far as I know, with all the means necessary for outfitting and promoting the new orphan houses. Six years and eight months I have been day by day, generally several times a day, asking the Lord for the needed means for this enlargement of the orphan work, which, according to calculations made in the spring of 1861, appeared to be about fifty thousand pounds, but which at a later date was found to be about fifty-eight thousand pounds: I have now received this amount in total. I praise and magnify the Lord for putting the expansion of the work on my heart, and for giving me courage and faith for it; and above all, for sustaining my faith day by day without wavering. When the last portion of the money was received, I was no more assured concerning the endeavor than I was when I had not received a single donation toward this large sum. I was at the beginning, after once having ascertained His mind, through patient and heart-searching waiting upon God, as fully assured that He would bring it about as if the two houses, with their hundreds of orphans occupying them, had already been standing before me.

"I would like to make a few remarks here for the sake of young believers in connection with this subject: (1) Be slow to take new steps in the Lord's service, or in your business, or in regard to your families: weigh everything well; weigh all in the light of the Holy Scriptures and in the fear of God. (2) Seek to have no will of your own, in order to ascertain the mind of God regarding any steps you propose to take, so that you can honestly say you are willing to do the will of God, if He will only instruct you. (3) When you have found out what the will of God is, seek for His help, and seek it earnestly, perseveringly, patiently, believingly, expectantly; and you will surely in His own time and way obtain it.

"To suppose that we have difficulty only about money would be a mistake: there occur hundreds of other wants and difficulties. It is a rare thing that a day passes without some problem or some need; but often there are many of these met and overcome in the same day. Our universal remedy is prayer and faith, and we have never been disappointed. Patient, persevering, believing prayer, offered up to God in the name of the Lord Jesus, has always, sooner or later, brought the blessing. I do not despair, by God's grace, of obtaining any blessing provided I can be sure it would be for some real good and for the glory of God."